AUTHENTIC EVERYDAY DRESS OF THE RENAISSANCE

All 154 Plates from the "Trachtenbuch"

Christoph Weiditz

DOVER PUBLICATIONS, INC.
New York

Bibliographical Note

Authentic Everyday Dress of the Renaissance: All 154 Plates from the "Trachtenbuch" is a republication of *Das Trachtenbuch des Christoph Weiditz*, as described in the Publisher's Note.

Library of Congress Cataloging-in-Publication Data

Weiditz, Christoph, ca. 1500–1559.
    [Trachtenbuch des Christoph Weiditz von seinen Reisen nach Spanien (1529) und den Niederlanden (1531/32). English]
    Authentic everyday dress of the Renaissance : all 154 plates from the "Trachtenbuch" / Christoph Weiditz.
            p.   cm.
    Reproduces the English text only from the trilingual edition published in Berlin in 1927 by de Gruyter.
    Includes bibliographical references.
    ISBN 0-486-27975-8 (pbk.)
    1. Costume—Europe—History. 2. Renaissance. I. Title.
GT509.W4513   1994
391′.094′09031—dc20   93-44628
                                                                          CIP

Manufactured in the United States of America
Dover Publications, Inc., 31 East 2nd Street, Mineola, N.Y. 11501

PUBLISHER'S NOTE

In 1927, Verlag von Walter de Gruyter & Co., Berlin and Leipzig, published *Das Trachtenbuch des Christoph Weiditz von seinen Reisen nach Spanien (1529) und den Niederlanden (1531/32)*, edited by Dr. Theodor Hampe, a director of the Germanic National Museum in Nuremberg, where the manuscript was located. The text appeared in German, English and Spanish, and 41 of the plates were reproduced in color. With the exception of a few tacit corrections, the original English text is here reproduced unaltered. Each page of the Dover edition contains two of the plates of the de Gruyter edition. Although the plate numbers for the most part conform to those used by de Gruyter, in some instances they have been altered to accommodate the change in format.

INTRODUCTION

Heinrich Droege, the student of costumes and in particular the connoisseur of the rich treasures of the Franz von Lipperheide costume-library, who died a few years ago, all too soon, begins his small but fundamental treatise concerning "The costume-books of the 16th century" with the remark that "the most interesting epoch for the literature of the costume-books is the period from the appearance in the year 1562 of the oldest work of this kind known to us up to the end of the 16th century."[1]

This dictum can be accepted only conditionally. It is true that the study of national costumes first became a special branch of science through the appearance and the circulation of French and Italian copper engravings and woodcuts dealing with these matters, and it is naturally of great interest to observe with what zeal this new territory was developed and extended, and that instead of accepting indiscriminately and uncritically the old ideas, one now began with increasing knowledge to look into dependable sources and reports.

It is of no less interest to investigate the foundations upon which the structure of the history of national costumes gradually arose in the second half of the 16th century, and to note the active and even passionate interest exhibited even in the preceding decades in the different countries and parts of the earth for the many varieties of costumes and for their development—an interest which formed the foundation of the whole literature dealing with this subject, in other words, for the success for the costume-books that followed. The 15th century and the first years of the 16th century, with their steadily increasing production of the most valuable velvet and silk fabrics, with the steadily increasing splendour of the Burgundian Court and the Italian Dynasties, which competed with each other in outward display—in short, with the joyous pleasure in colours and with the unfailing taste of the early Renaissance shown by all cultivated peoples of old Europe in all affairs of the daily life—this everywhere richly flowering period was calculated, as hardly any other, not merely to sharpen the artist's eye for the outward appearance of mankind, but also to awaken the appreciation of the most extended circles along the same line. If we observe the development of painting on wood from the end of the 14th to the beginning of the 16th century—a development almost entirely confined to church art—we see a continuous increase in the attention paid to the costumes and to the care with which all details of these are carried out, from the bonnet, the silk hat and numerous other head-coverings down to the most various kinds of foot-wear. At the beginning of the new epoch this tendency makes itself manifest already in frequent works and even in whole series, in which the chief weight is laid on details of costume which therefore can in large part be regarded as purely costume pictures. To these belong many of the charming finely delineated drawings of Albrecht Duerer and Hans Holbein the Younger, both of whom may already have conceived the idea of a costume-book. To these belong also the dancing bridal couples of Aldegrever or Hans Leonhard Schaeufelein and others, and, at a certain distance from these, also the earliest genealogical books with the still so naive representation of ancestors

---

[1] Cf Beiträge zur Bücherkunde und Philologie, August Wilmanns zum 25. März 1903 gewidmet (Leipzig, Harrassowitz, 1903), p. 429—444.

bearing their coats of arms, the memoirs of the Augsburg dandies Matthaeus and Veit Konrad Schwarz, who always had their picture taken every time a new fashion came up, and many more. Indeed, Enea Vico's great series of copper cuts showing 70 Spanish and 29 other national costumes, which also reach back to the first half of the 16th century and in part served as a basis for the oldest real costume-book ("Recueil de la diversité des habits qui sont de présent en usage tant es pays d'Europe, Asie, Affrique et Isles sauvages," Paris 1562), as also for the book of the Italian Ferdinando Bertelli, which appeared only a year later ("Omnium fere gentium nostrae aetatis habitus, nunquam antehac aediti," Venice, 1563), can as a whole be regarded as constituting a costume-book by themselves.

The complete titles of the two costume-works of 1562 and 1563 cited by me appear to show that in that epoch, so powerfully influenced by humanism and by great and successful voyages of discovery, the conception of such a complete collection and publication of pictures of costumes obviously extended, if not precisely over the whole world, nevertheless far over other lands and seas. The difficulty and expense of extended travel, and the national character and economic dependence of most of the German and as well as of the Italian and French masters of the Renaissance, may also have been one reason why, despite hard work and splendid beginnings, such collections did not appear till comparatively late.

We find one of these important beginnings also in a work which I here introduce for the first time to the literature of the elder costume-works, and which can be designated as the earliest of these. It is a modest quarto volume which was presented by Dr. Johann N. Egger, district physician in Freyung near Passau, on the Bavarian-Austrian border, on April 14, 1868, to the library of the Germanic National Museum of Nuremberg. It has been impossible to trace the ownership of this book further back than Dr. Egger. It bears the library's number "Hs. 22474. 4." It contains 154 pages of heavy paper, almost like cardboard, which has a width of about 150 mm. and a length of 198—200 mm. It is most likely that these sheets were not originally assembled in book form, although it is possible, as we shall see, that they may have been intended to form the basis for a work of woodcuts which had been planned but had not been carried out completely. The book shows costumes of the better and lower classes, folk types and scenes from the public and home life especially of Spain, but also of the Netherlands, Italy and France, and furthermore, by way of example or comparison, of Germany, England, Ireland and Portugal. The pictures are pen drawings, boldly executed, water-coloured, and in part with raised gold and silver lines. Although the assumption regarding the original purpose of these pages is of course arbitrary, there is much reason to wonder whether the volume contains all the pictures that originally belonged to it, and it is to be hoped that, with this book as a starting point, further pictures of costumes from the hand of the same artist may be found in museums and private collections.

For the present, however, we must be satisfied with the 154 pages of our codex, which are all painted only on one side, but in many cases two of which have been used for the reproduction of a large scene containing many figures. All these pages and double pages were then at the end of the 18th century—this is the only thing that we can say concerning the history of this book— roughly assembled in a simple, entirely undecorated pasteboard covering, which had a solid pigskin back and the sides of which were covered with a marbled paper. The pages were unfortunately thrown together just as it happened, for the order in which they appear in the "Hs. 22474. 4" gives no evidence of any plan whatever. On the contrary, somebody who once owned them appears to have shuffled the pages like a deck of cards before having them bound together. But nevertheless we must be grateful to him for having them bound, for they would otherwise hardly have been preserved in such number and at the same place. But there was one sadder thing. The owner was so careless and indifferent as to give the bookbinder no directions for doing the work. The result is that these sheets, which were undoubtedly much more stately and had broad margins, were not only not mounted where it was necessary because of their being creased, but all of them were also trimmed, in the course of which some small parts of the texts above or below the pictures were cut off. The sheets, which probably lay around for a long time unbound, have also suffered all kinds of other damage through being marked up by children, and specially by mildew, small rents which were patched up, and even by bookworms. All in all, however, the state of preservation can be designated as excellent, and the drawings themselves have lost almost nothing of their freshness, nor have their mainly bright colours suffered at all to speak of. The thoroughly artistic character of the style, which flows easily and inclines to coarseness rather than to subtleness, and the direct appeal which the greatest part of the pictures makes on us are such that this old costume-book still exercises a strong effect today.

In view of these excellencies of our manuscript, which have been only touched upon lightly above, it is really astonishing that the codex has attracted virtually no attention whatever up to the present time. These excellencies will be seen more plainly later on, and above all, in my opinion, in the coloured photographic prints made with such great care by the Munich Art Institutions of J. B. Obernetter and by Wolff & Son. As a partial explanation of why the codex has been neglected it may be pointed out that the study of costumes was carried on up to only a few years ago in a somewhat dilettante manner, and that a really deep and scientific study was only undertaken a short time ago. Little of fundamental value, particularly for special questions or local developments, can be gained from the excellent Weiss, Racinet, Koehler, Hottenroth—whom one could hardly get along without—and from so many other books and their prints. Another reason for the failure to discover this comprehensive book so long can perhaps be found in the unusual popularity of the Germanic Museum, which resulted, especially in the flourishing years before the war, in bringing together such a great collection of the most different kinds and so many libraries and archives that the comparatively small number of employees could not even think of a thorough arranging or publishing of everything valuable and important. And hence this manuscript lay open for many years in a cabinet in the department for prints and manuscripts, so that its importance was not recognized. Not until a complete rearrangement of this department of the Library came, together with the inaugurating of instructive courses in the history of costumes, was this long neglected codex more carefully examined, with the result that its great historical and cultural value was established.

The realisation of its value was suddenly greatly increased by establishing the identity of the artist who can be regarded with the greatest probability as the one who made all the drawings of the volume. His appearance could not but throw a new and hitherto unimagined light upon the old manuscript. Even Dr. Karl Frommann, the Germanist and highly learned and ingenious critic, formerly librarian and second director of the Germanic Museum, who carefully catalogued the book immediately after its discovery, did not discover the name of the master, although he could have found this in the codex itself. It is true, however, that the darkness could only be penetrated after Georg Habich's pioneer investigations had completely solved the mystery which had long concealed the personality of one of the most prominent of the makers of medallions of the Augsburg Renaissance. Habich succeeded in identifying that important artist who had up to that time been known as the "unknown Augsburg wood-carver," and also, because of the most characteristic and historically most important medallions, as the "Dantiscus" or "Cortezmeister," with the goldsmith Christoph Weiditz.[2] This gave a quite unhoped for possibility of securing a clear conception of that personality who is pictured on page 78 of our manuscript (cf. plate I). "Thus Stoffel Weiditz voyaged over seas with Kolman Helmschmied," was read on the text complementing this picture,

        [2] Yearbook of the Royal Prussian Art Collections, vol. 34 (Berlin 1913), pages 1 — 35, with numerous illustrations Ibid., Die deutschen Medailleure des XVI. Jahrhunderts (Halle 1916), pages 30 — 36.

and the connection of the medallion maker with our book became immediately plain, because we know from the documents and also from a group of medallions collected by Habich that Stoffel Weiditz made a journey in the year 1529 to the court of Kaiser Charles V in Spain. The mention of Colman Helmschmied would also in itself have shown the connection with Augsburg, for this name can only refer to one of the two famous Augsburg plate-armourers who were frequently engaged by the Spanish Court—namely, either Koloman Colman, called Helmschmied, or his son, Desiderius Colman Helmschmied. The father, a son of the also well known Imperial Court artist Lorenz Colman, was born about 1470 in Augsburg, and died there in 1532.[3] From a letter of Jean Hannart, the diplomat of Charles V, dated at Nuremberg on March 14, 1524, it is seen that the Kaiser then desired to attract him to Spain for some time. However, the master made the excuse that he had a wife and several children, and furthermore that he was engaged for two years in advance upon work for princes and noblemen. It is a fact that he was at that time, and as Wendelin Boeheim's investigations have shown,[4] up to the year 1530, busily engaged for the Court of Mantua. It may be questioned whether the aging master would still in 1529 under these circumstances have found the time and bodily energy for the difficult trip to the Imperial Court. I incline to doubt it, and assume rather that he sent his son Desiderius, who had in the meantime become a young man, and who now, together with Christoph Weiditz, undertook the long journey and probably had to bring to the Kaiser the great suit of armour which is today preserved in Madrid, unfortunately no longer complete, and which, as Wendelin Boeheim says, was called the armour "with the wild animals," and which must have been completed in Augsburg by the father, as his most important work, for Charles V soon after 1525. A medallion still exists, dated 1555, showing Desiderius Colman Helmschmied, who later, as imperial armourer, achieved still greater fame than his father and grandfather. This medallion from the hand of a still unknown artist, the "Master of Heidegger," as Habich calls him, shows Desiderius at the age of 42 years ("aet. 42 iar d. 26. Sept."). According to this he would have been born in 1513 and would have been in 1529 only 16 years old. However, the fact that his name appears as early as 1534 in the Augsburg taxrolls shows that he came early to maturity and stood on his own feet. He died in 1575.

However, the question as to whether Weiditz is actually to be regarded as the master of the costume-book is more important than the question as to whether the elder or the younger Colman Helmschmied was the travelling companion. The fact that he is mentioned in the superscription on sheet 78 (plate I) in the third person would seem rather to point to a different hand, and hence it is possible that one of the ingenious plate-armourers or perhaps even a third person comes into question here. The relations with Spain and with the Imperial Court, which play such a prominent part in the costume-book, would apply equally to each of the two Colmans.

Several indications, however, point decidedly to Christoph Weiditz as the creator of the drawings. Chief among these and almost decisive is the reproduction of Ferdinand Cortez in full figure on sheet 77 (cf. plate IV) of the costume-book, a drawing which undoubtedly served the "Cortez master" as the model for the half-length picture on his famous portrait medallion.[5] It is most improbable that an artist of Weiditz's rank, who obviously met Cortez in Spain in 1529, would not himself have conceived this picture of the Conqueror of Mexico. In addition to this comes the strong love for costumes and ornaments which we find in Christoph Weiditz, and which, indeed, was only natural for a maker of medallions with keen powers of observation. Finally, I desire to direct particular attention to the very obvious woodcut character of the drawings in the costume-book, as to which I have already observed that they were very possibly intended to be carried out and made public in this technique.

[3] Concerning the three Augsburg armourers Colman, named Helmschmied, cf. Wendelin Boeheim, Meister der Waffenschmiedekunst vom 14. bis ins 18. Jahrhundert (Berlin 1897) pages 38—51.

[4] Ibid. page 44.

[5] Cf. the vignette on page 20 of this treatise. The medallion is also reproduced in the yearbook of the Prussian Art Collections (vol. 34, plate IV, 7).

The decisive lines, the shadings, which have an entirely woodcut character, and the strong outlines could not but suggest this. Moreover, we know that Christoph Weiditz had from the beginning the closest relations with the wood-carver. It can even be assumed that he received his first impulses and training in a wood-carver's shop. This assumption is strengthened by the graphic character of the reverse of many of the medallions, which, moreover, now and then, for instance in the analogous representation of horses, appears to show a direct relationship with the drawings of the costume-book. In addition to this it is extremely probable that Weiditz returned in the last decades of his life to the art of wood-carving, and that the woodcuts in the Augsburg Genealogy of 1550, signed at the time with a "C W", came from his hand. And these woodcuts, in the strength and certainty with which they are made, betray a near relationship with our drawings. We shall later have occasion to refer again to the life and activities of the master.

Hence the authorship of Christoph Weiditz for our costume-book can hardly be seriously doubted. Thus we are quite justified, in the rearrangement of the different sheets that has been made for the present edition of the manuscript, in placing his self-portrait in sea traveller's costume (sheet 78) in plate I at the very beginning of the whole work, and the only question that now remains to be answered is how the really astonishing text that accompanies it came into existence.

No serious objection could be made to the assumption that Weiditz himself chose this accompanying text. It is not at all unusual in the case of self-portraits, and particularly when these are intended for publication, for the artist to refer to himself in the third person. In the case at hand, however, the matter appears to have been much different and more complicated.

The city archives at Augsburg still contain several documents, obviously written by the artist himself and signed with his full name, which refer to Weiditz's quarrels with the Augsburg goldsmiths. Among these is a petition to the City Council from the year 1530, which is accompanied by a copy of the "Imperial Freedom" conferred upon him by Charles V, but the character of the writing varies so greatly from certain letters addressed in the year 1554 to the Council and to the committee of the goldsmiths that one would hardly believe—although one is at the same time compelled to believe—that both these earlier and later documents were written by Christoph Weiditz himself. However, the Renaissance laid great stress on the beauty and variety both of handwriting and of types, and especially in the case of an artist like Weiditz, who as goldsmith and maker of medallions and also as engraver, undoubtedly paid great attention to the art of writing, it can fairly be assumed that he was able at the same time to employ different methods of writing—in 1530 a flowing cursive, but in 1553 a stiffer, more carefully formed and ornamental writing which approached printing.

The writing used in our costume-book, which, however, and also because of the paper used, is to be regarded as some two decades earlier, has a certain resemblance only to this later writing. Hence the possibility that Weiditz himself did the writing is not at all to be regarded as out of question. But certain other indications nevertheless are opposed to this assumption. On the one hand, the texts accompanying the pictures of Ferdinand Cortez (plate IV) and of Andrea Doria (plate V) appear to show that these inscriptions were added a few years after the drawings were conceived and first executed, and that the text originally, that is, in 1529, probably was different. This will be discussed again briefly when the different plates are dealt with. On the other side, however, serious orthographic and syntactical mistakes, and above all the completely corrupted and at times hardly understandable passages found throughout all the inscriptions, show most plainly that we have here changes or additions made by some ignorant person, and occasionally quite arbitrarily. Matters of this kind were not taken too seriously in those days.

In my opinion the costume-book came into existence in the following manner: From his Spanish trip in 1529, and also at the end of 1530 or the beginning of 1531, after he had, as we must assume from the medallions made at that time, followed the Kaiser to the Netherlands, Christoph Weiditz brought well filled sketchbooks back to Augsburg. On the different sheets he wrote hasty inscriptions or explanations, readable by other persons with difficulty, and he may possibly also have indicated at first by brief notes the colours to be used. With these sketches as a basis he then, in the period of leisure following his extended trip, undertook with his own hand— the pronounced woodcut character of the drawings shows this—the careful execution of the sheets with pen and brush and with colours. He then had the inscriptions added according to his own conceptions by a professional scribe, who knew how to make the flourishing initials, although unfortunately in part very badly. It is possible that this good man then used on sheet 78, plate I, the third personal form.

A more exact consideration of the probable production and origin of the Weiditz drawings and of the manner in which they were arranged later will be given in the following first main part of the introduction. Here, however, attention is to be directed particularly to the reason why our comment on the costume-book could merely consist of a brief introduction to the book itself and also to its introduction into literature. Lack of space in itself made it impossible at this time to take up thoroughly the history of national costumes, to say nothing of dealing thoroughly with the handwriting. In addition to this, a more exact knowledge of existing handwritten manuscripts, especially those in Spanish libraries, would have been required than was possible at this time. For although the previous publications of the works of old painting art and plastic in Spain, Carderera's "Iconografia española" or the works of Emanuel von Cuendias, Valerian von Loga, August L. Mayer and others afford valuable material dealing with the history of costumes, this material is confined almost altogether to the costumes, and especially the elaborate festival costumes of the upper classes, whereas the drawings of Christoph Weiditz in the main give us an opportunity to see broad masses of the Spanish people at the time of the early Renaissance—one can perhaps say, for the first time—at their work and in the other activities of their daily life.

And we should undoubtedly have to turn to Spain first of all if we wished to look for those artistic and literary sources of our master, which, as we shall see, must in all probability be assumed for certain groups of his pictures of costumes. For the German of today, however, such investigations, which we shall on the whole do best to leave in the hands of the Spanish themselves, would undoubtedly prove to demand too much time and too much expense, and would also unduly delay the publication of the manuscript. Hence it can only be said at this time on the basis of investigations such in particular as those which a young art historian, Fritz Kriegbaum, was good enough to make for me during several months which he spent in study in the libraries and collections in Spain, that not even the prototype of those Weiditz sheets for which we can assume with great probability that certain patterns already existed—these make up, however, only a small part of the total contents of our codex—has thus far probably not been published or even become known.

Neither in the National Library in Madrid (Custodian, Angel Sánchez Rivero) nor in the library of the Escorial (Director, Padre Guillermo Antolin), could such a preliminary work or prototype of our costume-book be found. Nor has any source from which it may have come become known thus far even to the best authority on the history of Spanish costumes, Don Juan Comba y Garcia, Professor at the Musical Conservatory in Madrid, who has been working for years at the great "Historia del traje en España" and, as former court painter, has in pursuance of this work studied the pictorial manuscripts of many Spanish libraries and made copies of them.

Don Juan Comba further points out that it has been especially difficult to secure for the work planned by him material covering the first half of the 16th century, since both drawings and miniatures throw almost no light whatever on that period. Hence it is to be hoped that Weiditz's work will, when published, do much to fill this gap — quite apart from its great cultural and historical value.

Hence I content myself with introducing the faithful reproduction of the codex simply through a short biography of our artist, together with a characterisation of his costume-book, an indication of its place in the literature dealing with this subject, and also a brief comment on the different tables, to which is added a description of the colours used in the original drawings.

My hearty thanks are due to all those who have assisted me in the publication of this work with word and deed—in addition to Fritz Kriegbaum, particularly Professor Dr. Adolf Schulten of the University of Erlangen, the prominent authority on old and new Spain, Dr. August L. Mayer of Munich, the thorough student of Spanish art, and the officials and employees who were consulted in preparing the work at hand. May this old costume-book which I present here give a new and powerful impetus to cultural science, making its development steadily richer, and form a new bond between German and Spanish science for a harmonious cooperation for achieving the common high aims.

Nuremberg, in the summer of 1925.

THEODOR HAMPE.

FIRST PART

THE ARTIST AND THE WORK

Although Christoph Weiditz did his chief work in Augsburg, he appears to have been born in Strassburg, at that time quite as German a city as Augsburg. At the end of the 15th century or the beginning of the 16th century, the period in which he appears to have been born, there were several artists of the name of Weiditz in Southwestern Germany. There was a sculptor named Bartholomäus Widitz of Meissen, who became a master in Strassburg in 1467; there was also that Johann Wydyz whose name appears on a carved altar in the Münster at Freiburg in Baden, dated 1505 and depicting the Adoration of the Magi, and further Hans Weydtz, the draftsman and probably also the carver of the woodcuts of Otto Brunfels' book on herbs, "Herbarum vivae eicones." [6] In the preface to the German edition of this book (Strassburg, Johann Schott, 1530—36) it is expressly declared that the illustrations were "cut and counterfeited by the highly renowned master Hans Weiditz of Strassburg," and it must naturally be assumed from this wording that this artist had already distinguished himself by other works. The thesis has been maintained that he was identical with the formerly unknown "Petrarch master," the highly gifted and imaginative draftsman of the woodcuts of the German edition of the Petrarch "Trostspiegel," which was published by Heinrich Steiner in Augsburg in 1531, and of the woodcuts of other German editions of works of the Italian poet. This thesis, however, has recently been severely shaken by the investigations and critical studies of Th. Musper and Buchner, although it can still not be regarded as completely destroyed. [7]

The solution of this problem can not greatly interest us here, since it plays only a subordinate part in connection with the question of the descent and development of Christoph Weiditz. For the woodcut character and the narrative tone that characterise the figures on the reverse of many of his memorial coins, and which, as in the case of the medal made in honour of the Strassburg Humanist Johannes Huttichius von Idstein in 1523, appear to betray the influence of the Petrarch master, whether this was Hans Weiditz or Peter Zan, or somebody else, could solely have come from a knowledge and study of that artist's woodcuts in the early Augsburg and later Strassburg prints. On the other hand, however, it would be possible to secure very respectable support for the shaken Weiditz hypothesis from this close artistic relationship, which Habich has repeatedly emphasised, and also from the fact that the woodcutting activities of the Petrarch master are later transferred entirely to Strassburg, where it is proved by the records that a "Hans Widitz, Painter," was still living in 1565, whereas the name is never found in the city records of Augsburg.

Furthermore, the earliest medals which we possess from the artist indicate Strassburg as the home or place of birth of Christoph Weiditz. Like the medal of Johannes Huttichius, the medals of Christoph Stettle (1523), Heinrich von Eppendorf, Jacob von Molsheim, Matthias Steffli, Elogius Honnu, Jörg Brun, Friedrich Prechter (all of 1524) and others point to very close connections

---

[6] For questions of genealogy, particularly regarding Hans Weiditz, cf. Heinrich Röttinger, Hans Weiditz the Petrarch Master (Strassburg 1904), page 17 et seq. and page 23 et seq. Max J. Friedlaender, Woodcuts by Hans Weiditz (Berlin 1922), page 6 et seq.

[7] Cf. Ernst Buchner, "Der Petrarkameister als Maler, Miniator und Zeichner," in the memorial for Heinrich Wölfflin (Munich 1924), page 209 et seq The unprinted Munich dissertation of Th. Musper is cited by Buchner in note 6.

with Augsburg or the rest of Alsace, and during building operations at No. 4 Ochsengasse at Strassburg the clay mould was found of a Christoph Weiditz medal to the "honourable Jörg Betscholt, Vicarius at the old St. Peter's," as the person represented is designated in the Strassburg city records.[8]

Hence we can probably assume with Habich, Friedlaender and others, that our master was born about 1500 in Strassburg as son of the wood-carver Johann, who himself can be regarded as a son of the sculptor Bartholomäus, and as the younger brother of the draftsman and form-cutter Hans Weiditz, and that in this city, probably in his brother's workshop, he was exposed above all to the influence of the graphic art of the Petrarch Master, and especially to the influence of the master's illustrations for Johannes Huttichius's treatise on Roman Imperial coins (Imperatorum Romanorum libellus, Strassburg 1525). It is possible that it was precisely this work that caused him at first to abandon the art of wood-carving and devote his entire attention to medals. His real schooling as portraitist must, however, nevertheless have been received in these years in a Strassburg sculptor's workshop, for when he appears in Augsburg in 1526, the technique of his medals of Augsburg personalities, which assume the most prominent place in the following years and throw most light also on his own biography, indicates the already finished master. Then, however, we see him in matters of style, or rather of taste, come more and more under the influence of Friedrich Hagenauer, who also came from Strassburg and settled in Augsburg at almost the same time. In certain cases, indeed, we are compelled to assume a close cooperation of Christoph Weiditz with Hagenauer, just as Habich has proved such close connection in a case of a medal in 1527 of the important aquarelle painter Narziss Renner, the master of the Augsburg "Geschlechtertanz", who devoted his chief attention to costume motives. The obverse of this medal, declares Habich, is "a good example of the soft, broad delineation of form" of Christoph Weiditz, while the short inscription on the reverse shows unmistakably Hagenauer's hand and contains even the twining leaves so characteristic of this artist. "Later on Hagenauer also made a portrait of the splendid colourist, but without attaining the convincing vitality of the Weiditz medal" (Habich). In the case of our master, however, it may have been precisely the acquaintance with Narziss Renner and his art that importantly furthered an inclination to sharp observation and precise reproduction of details and costume.

It is not necessary to devote any further attention to those men and women who had their portraits made by Christoph Weiditz during his first years in Augsburg, 1526—1528, such as Ulrich Rechlinger, the fanatical Protestant son of the Burgomaster; Jakob Herbrot, the Burgomaster of the Guilds; the Augsburg goldsmiths Ottmar Widenmann and Cyprian Schaller, the Felicitas Lucasin, Katharina Meringer and all the others — some 20 to 25 medals come from these years. All that we are interested in here is in establishing the fact that precisely these medals prove with certainty that our master moved from Strassburg to Augsburg.

The first person whose portrait was made in the following years (1529—1532) is believed by Habich to have been that Johannes Dantiscus, the boxwood model of whose medal is preserved in the Berlin coin cabinet, and the first medals of Christoph Mülich were made in the same period. Both Johann van Hoeven (Latinized, "de Curiis"), who called himself Dantiscus after his birthplace Danzig (born 1485, died 1548 as Bishop of Ermland in Frauenberg), and Christoph Mülich, who as one of the business representatives of the Fugger firm in Italy was living most of the time in Milan and Rome, but who occasionally spent some time in Augsburg, enjoyed close relations with the Imperial Court. Dantiscus in particular at that time spent several years in the vicinity of the Emperor, and also carried on the correspondence with Mülich in which, among other things, reference is made to the medals by "Christoff Pildhawer," which, according to the documents preserved in the city archives of Augsburg, can not have meant anybody else than Christoph Weiditz.

---

[8] Cf. R. Forrer, in the Archiv für Medaillen- und Plakettenkunde I (1913—14) page 27 et seq.

It is possible that Weiditz at that time (1529) had a hostile reception from the Augsburg goldsmiths because he had served his apprenticeship in a sculptor's or form-cutter's workshop, for the goldsmiths regarded the "counterfitting," the making of medals "of goldsmith's work," as it is called, as the privilege of their guild. This may have been one of the reasons why he accepted an invitation from Johannes Dantiscus to come to the latter at the Court of Charles V in Spain, in order to secure, with the help of the influential patron, the imperial decree protecting him against his opponents. He might have learned that Colman Helmschmied was planning the same trip and thus accompanied him. However, this is a matter of conjecture. But it is certain that the long foreign voyages of Christoph Weiditz, of which the persons whose portrait medals were made in that period give evidence, took place in the years mentioned (1529—1532), and that he later made use against the goldsmiths of the imperial letter which he, as he himself reports, "having come to Spain, received there from the Roman Imperial Majesty, our most gracious lord." It is true that this Imperial letter, which is still preserved in the municipal documents ("We, Charles the Fifth, by the grace of God Roman Emperor," etc.) is dated at Augsburg on November 7, 1530. It is possible that Weiditz was also at that time, together with Dantiscus, who had been appointed Bishop of Kulm in 1530, in the court retinue of the Emperor, whom he undoubtedly accompanied to the Netherlands at the end of 1530 or the beginning of 1531. The return trip brought him in 1532 to Nuremberg, where he appears to have spent some time.

Numerous splendid models of persons whose portraits he made furnish dependable evidence of these trips. He executed the portrait of Ferdinand Cortez in Spain in 1529, of Heinrich von Eppendorf or Christoph Mülich among others in 1530 in Augsburg, of Ulrich Ehinger, Grand Admiral Adolph de Bourgogne of the Netherland fleet, Herr von Beveren, Charles de Solier, the French Minister at the English Court, and the Sieur de Morette in 1531 in the Netherlands. In like manner he could only have made the portraits of Franz Wernherr and his wife Clara of Nuremberg and of Hans and Anna Berchtold in Nuremberg in 1532. Indeed, in Georg Habich's words, "the Suevian bourgeoisie of the Imperial cities and the internationally constituted field courts of Charles V were the two poles of Christoph Weiditz's labours."

We shall come back later in the second part of this chapter to particular consideration of the Spanish trip of the artist and of his acquaintanceship and observations at the imperial court. It suffices here to note briefly that the assumption of a lengthy stay in the Netherlands finds considerable support in the space given in our costume-book to the representation of costumes and customs in Hennegau, Flanders, Holland, Seeland and Friesland. For the present we take up solely the later years of Christoph Weiditz's life.

At the outset we can follow only up until 1537 his activity as the maker of medals in Augsburg, where he probably lived for the next few years. Up to the date named a great number of splendidly worked out portraits of members of prominent South German families, in particular Suevian and Augsburg families, came from his busy hands. Then, however, this production appears to break off abruptly, and though in the following years several smaller groups of medals are found that show a close relationship with Christoph Weiditz's style, the obvious falling off of this art in comparison with the richness of this first highly creative decade, at least in the two last decades of his life, can not but be noticeable.

It is probable that this remarkable development has some connection with the strained relations between him and the Augsburg goldsmiths. Although he had on March 3, 1532, probably because of the imperial rescript, secured the right to work as sculptor, the goldsmiths opposed then as before his doing any kind of works of silver or gold, although the imperial "Grace and Freedom" had made such an occupation as master or apprentice solely dependent upon the creation of a masterpiece and upon the payment of the usual fees. The representatives of the goldsmiths, however, insisted that he must first serve his four years as apprentice, although he had already, as he declared in his petition, "made masterpieces enough, praise God." They refused also to make the necessary inspection of the silver used by him, incited his apprentices against him and otherwise persecuted him. It is true, however, that an upright and wise council protected the artist and his art. "It protects me in a fatherly manner," writes Weiditz himself, "and informed me that I could continue to do my work which redounds to the praise and fame of the city in general. I have done and am still doing such work as that His Roman Imperial and Royal Majesty has himself praised it and been pleased with it, as well as other princes and lords of German and foreign lands."[9] It appears also that this action of the council was at one time followed by a period of quiet of several years. In the years from 1550 to 1560, however, the old quarrel was renewed, but the records, which are badly preserved, give no clear indication as to how the matter ended.

In the meantime he had married Regina Forster and his modest means had continuously increased, as we can see in the Augsburg taxrolls, in which his name, without any statement of his occupation, appears for the first time in 1533. In 1549 he bought a house in the street called then as now "Herrenhäuser," moved from there in 1552 to another street "hinter den Predigern," but from 1552 up to his death he appears again as the owner of a house in the "Herrenhäuser," where he still paid his taxes in 1559. He must have died in the same year, for according to the Augsburg records dealing with the estates of decedents, the butcher Ludwig Schmidt was on August 1, 1559, appointed as guardian for a minor relative (step-brother or nephew) of Regina Forster, "in the place of Christoph Weiditz, goldsmith, deceased."[10] The other guardian, the sculptor Joachim Forster, the brother of Regina and brother-in-law of Christoph Weiditz, was at that time absent from Augsburg. In another place we read of him that he, too, like Weiditz, in contravention of the guild rules and against the protest of the goldsmiths, made all kinds of works of silver and gold, and it was probably the close relationship with this brother-in-law that brought about the renewed campaign of the goldsmiths against Weiditz. Furthermore, both also made "pictures" of clay, guilder's mass, marble and other stone, wood and iron. This note, which is taken from the records of the goldsmiths, seems to me to point toward many other small plastic works which, in part in joint labour with his brother-in-law, may have come from the hand of Christoph Weiditz, especially in the last two decades of his life, and which may indeed have been responsible in considerable part for the gradual increase of his prosperity. On the other hand, however, as has been pointed out before, it is by no means impossible that in the course of time and following further investigations, numerous other medals will be definitely established as coming from him. In individual cases our costume-book will also be able to furnish grounds for such ascriptions to him, and great hopes can certainly still be rested on more careful investigations of public and private collections in Spain. We know from various well preserved reports concerning the ordering and delivering of portrait medals that these were only seldom made in large quantities, and also that the modeller and the moulder were by no means always the same person. The models, which were the real artistic creation, were very frequently preserved and well cared for by the families whose members they represented, in order that, from time to time when special occasions made it desirable, the models could be used again for the casting of medals by means of the process called "Cire perdue".

In view of the manysidedness that characterised the sculptor and goldsmith Christoph Weiditz as a genuine master of the Renaissance, one can here, at the conclusion of the discussion of his life and work, again raise the question as to the degree in which he turned his attention in his later years also to drawings for wood-carvings or to wood-carvings themselves, and whether the "pictures" of the most varied material which are referred to in brief form by the document of 1554 already referred to, are not, with the exception of models for medals and the other woodcuts, perhaps less to be regarded as forms. This question presents itself particularly, as already briefly

[9] Exact text from the Augsburg archives   Cf. also Habich in the yearbook, 34, 27.
[10] Augsburg municipal archives.

mentioned, in connection with the book of genealogy published by the Augsburg clerk of council, Paul Hector Mair, the title of which was "Declaratio et Demonstratio omnium patricii loci atque ordinis Familiarum in laudatissima Augustae Vindelicorum Civitate." A new edition of this work appeared in print in 1550, in Augsburg, coming from the press of Melchior Kriechstein, 14 years after a Strassburg edition had been "printed by Christoffel Widitz and David Konnel." It consists of four parts and presents in whole-page woodcuts of small folio size 156 representatives of leading Augsburg families, both living and dead. These woodcuts, which present the figures in full length, often with fantastic armour, represent with few exceptions rather the representative members of the family, which are also repeatedly duplicated, than portraits of individual persons. On four of these sheets, one at the end of each separate part of the book, one finds the initials "C. W.", mainly alongside the always present coat-of-arms, and these initials without any doubt refer to Christoph Weiditz or Widitz, the printer and also the wood-carver. Habich has already assumed that they refer to our artist. Hence he then would have to be identical with the wood-carver Christoph Widitz who took up his residence in Strassburg in 1557 — that is, as Habich emphasises, precisely in the year in which the series of medals with certainty ascribable to our Weiditz abruptly ceases. Hence we shall have to assume a temporary return of the master to the city where he was probably born. Another thing that points to the authorship of our Weiditz is the almost exclusively profile position of the heads in the Augsburg book of genealogy, a position especially understandable in the case of an experienced maker of medals. The already mentioned similarity with our book, which is still more striking in the case of an old, coloured copy of the book of genealogy in the library of the Paul Wolfgang Merkel family foundation in the Germanic Museum — an artistic masterpiece in its careful execution, tasteful selection and richly embossed gold and silver colours — lends greater probability to this assumption. And hence, as long as no new discoveries compel another solution of the question, I must maintain that the two Christoffel Weiditz were identical. Moreover, the idea of a similar publication appears to have occurred to our master several years earlier while he was working on his costume-book.

In view of the sureness of line and the liveliness of the representation characterising the pictures of the costume-book, and still more the woodcuts of the Paul Hector Mair works, it would be a matter for wonder if other graphic works, particularly book paintings, were not discovered from the same trained hand. Among the documents of the Augsburg city library, however, I found only a few clues. However, my investigation was only a cursory one. The chief result of these investigations would be that our artist collaborated in another costume-book, "Memmorjbuch der Klaytung vnnd der visirung zum Himel vnd zum Fennlein," 1542, by "P.H.M.R.", that is, as shown by a notice at the end, "Paul Hector Mair, Ratsschreiber" (clerk of council), whom we should thus see again in close relationship with Christoph Weiditz. The first part of the manuscript, which deals with clothing, contains coloured representations, almost a whole page in size, of the "Provisioner" (municipal policemen), "Ainspenigen" (mounted police), foot and mounted militia, etc., in their costumes, or, as one could almost say, in their uniforms. Among these aquarelle paintings there are a few, especially the rude but imposing representation of a policeman on sheet 8a, that have a style greatly resembling that of the Weiditz costume-book in many respects, among others also in their method of presenting the earth. This pictorial handwriting also shows at the same time what a lively interest in questions regarding costumes had arisen in those days in Augsburg. Considerations of space make it impossible for us here to go into this matter in detail or to investigate other influences which our artist may have exercised or to which he may have been subjected. It is also to be hoped that as soon as the publication of the Weiditz costume-book makes it available to other investigators, a more careful investigation and comparison of the work in libraries and collections will uncover further relationships and lead to the finding of many further clues.

The period in which Christoph Weiditz undertook his trip to Spain, with, as we may fairly assume, Colman Helmschmied, was probably the most excited and changeable period that Europe has experienced. Events and undertakings of incalculable importance were condensed into a space of a few decades, and all of them were only too well calculated to disturb both minds and passions deeply. The firm faith and bold ambition of a Christopher Columbus, and then the daring voyages of discovery and conquest of the Spaniards and Portuguese, which rapidly opened up a vista into the new unknown world across the seas, marked the opening of this period which is so important for the development of the whole human race. And a short time before this the foundation of the Spanish kingdom had been laid in the Pyrenaean peninsula by the marriage of Ferdinand of Aragon with Isabella of Castile, a kingdom which came into actual existence in the following period with the succession to the throne of the 16-year-old grandson of Ferdinand and Isabella, through the conquest of Granada and the dethroning of the last Morisco king, then through the addition of the Kingdom of Navarra, and finally in making a united whole of these lands, to which there belonged further at that time Sardinia, Sicily, the Kingdom of Naples and the new immeasurable American possessions.

On the other hand Italy, despite all striving for unity, remained politically dissevered, the plaything of foreign discordant powers, and the German nation, which had ever sought for expansion more on intellectual territory, was split in two as the result of Luther's defiance to the Church of Rome. France felt herself ever more threateningly encircled by the Habsburg monarchy, particularly after the death of Maximilian I. His grandson, the young Spanish ruler, had also become German King and Roman Emperor, and France saw her sphere of influence and alleged rights being hampered and extinguished, now in Naples, now in Navarra, and now in the Duchy of Milan. These fears and this antagonism led to the wars between Charles V and Franz I, which, together with the Italian complications, with the increase of piracy under Chaireddin Barbarossa as a result of the entanglements and disagreements of the Mediterranean powers—60,000 people are said to have been led into slavery in Africa in the one year 1531—with the horrors of the peasant war, with the religious wars following this, and with the Turkish invasions, prevented Middle Europe from coming to a peaceful settlement for decades.

In the year 1528 Ferdinand Cortez, the great conqueror, had returned to the home land as viceroy of "New Spain," in order to defend himself before Charles V against the charges made against him by the "Audiencia" (court of New Spain). He not only brought fabulous treasures with him from Mexico and laid them at the foot of his imperial master, but he was also attended by a following of Indians. Cortez's services to the throne of Spain were soon rewarded by his elevation to the rank of count and by the granting of lands in Mexico.

Almost at the same time the military situation between France and Charles V had been altered in favour of the latter by the unexpected action of the great Genoese Admiral Andreas Doria, who abandoned Franz I and went over to the Emperor. Doria had seized Genoa for Charles and had then at the beginning of August in the following year followed the call of his imperial master to Spain in order to make preparations for the long contemplated transfer of the ruler and his army to Italy. The first task was to restore the superior might of the Emperor in Italy and then order had to be brought into German affairs, which had become steadily more confused and had long required the presence of the ruler. Then a campaign must be undertaken against Sultan Soliman the Magnificent, who was even then preparing to besiege Vienna with an army of 250,000 men.

Up to this time the plan of a new campaign had not been carried out because of the difficulty of financing it, a difficulty which probably was due to a lack of faith in the success of the enterprise. But after the Emperor's prospects had been improved beyond all expectations by the decisive step of the great admiral, the money question was gradually brought nearer to a satisfactory solution. In agreement with Doria, Charles had chosen the harbour of Barcelona as the place of embarkation, and had, as early as March 19, 1529, summoned the legislative assemblies of the principalities of Catalonia to come to Barcelona in the middle of April. These assemblies, after the Kaiser himself had arrived on April 30, had also made an appropriation of 250,000 Barcelonese pounds. At the same time a fleet of more than 150 ships had been assembled which, quite apart from Doria's galleys, were capable of taking on board 2,000 mounted troups and 12,000 foot soldiers.

As a result of these preparations for war, the powers that were hostile to the Emperor endeavoured to secure a speedy peace. Peace was concluded as early as the end of June, 1529, in Barcelona with Pope Clemens VII, who had formerly been an ally of France, and peace was concluded in Cambrai at the beginning of August between France and the Emperor as the result of the zealous efforts of King Franz's mother, Luise of Savoy, and of Margarete of Austria, the aunt of Charles V.

And thus, when Doria's galleys entered the harbour of Barcelona to take the Emperor on board, it was possible for him to embark with light heart on the richly decorated and equipped admiral's ship for the trip to Italy and to the Empire from which he had been absent for nine years. On August 12 he landed in Genoa, where he was received with vast pomp and was honoured and welcomed with great festivals. The first months were devoted, in now completely renewed agreement with the Pope, to the setting in order of Italian affairs. Elaborate feasts and exaggerated demonstrations of loyalty marked his progress, and Charles would have been glad to remain longer in Italy if his brother Ferdinand in Germany had not continuously urged upon him the necessity of a speedy intervention in German quarrels and religious matters.

On January 21, 1530, writing from Bologna, where "the ruler of the Indies" a month later received from the hands of the Pope the crown of Lombardy and the imperial crown, he convoked the Reichstag to meet at Augsburg on April 8. In April the imperial train started for Germany over the Brenner, but not until June 15, after long and elaborate stays in Innsbruck and Munich, did the Emperor reach Augsburg, where on the following day, June 16, he took part in the celebration of Corpus Christi and remained until November 23 among the German princes and legates assembled for the Reichstag. On that date he started for the Netherlands. In December he meets his brother in Cologne and presides there over the first assembly of the electors, at which on January 5 Ferdinand was elected Roman King. On January 11 followed the coronation of Ferdinand in Aachen. On January 15 the Emperor left the city and reached Brussels at the end of January, to which city he then summoned the Estates of the Netherlands. At the beginning of the following spring he returned to Germany to be present at the Regensburg Reichstag.

How does the itinerary of our Christoph Weiditz fit in with this imperial itinerary? The medals themselves have already given us certain clues, and the costume-book furnishes additional ones, although, indeed, the course of his journeys is here also not clearly to be ascertained. The utter lack of any system in the costume-book already referred to, or, more properly speaking, the form and condition in which it has come down to us, is responsible for the fact that we are here mainly dependent upon surmises. On the other hand, however, many of the events and relationships of the great world which we have just briefly glanced at are reflected in the Weiditz work, and an extended connection of the artist with the imperial camp, together with Dantiscus, who was during these years mainly in the immediate surroundings of Charles V, is rendered more probable by the persons whose portraits were made in these years and also by our manuscript.

I am almost inclined to assume that the two travellers, Christoph Weiditz and Colman Helmschmied, did not join the imperial army and court at Barcelona, but that they joined the court while it was still in Castile, probably in Toledo or Valladolid. It may be assumed that Colman Helmschmied carried out his commission there, and it is possible also that many of those Weiditz medals which we must ascribe with greater or less probability to Spain were made there—particularly those of Johannes Dantiscus, two of which are dated 1529, the portrait of Ferdinando Cortez (1529), and perhaps also the undated medal of Emperor Charles V himself, whose portrait, as Habich points out, is of such lifelike character that one can hardly doubt that the Emperor sat for it personally.

Weiditz may then have followed the court through Castile and Aragon in the spring of 1529 to Barcelona. This conclusion seems justified by the picture of one of the imperial baggage waggons (plate IX) as well as that of the drummer at the entrance of the Emperor into a city (plate X). Apart from Granada and the Morisco and Basque provinces, to which we shall later devote special attention, Castile, next to Catalonia, plays by far the main part in the costume-book, so that we have reason to believe that our artist spent a considerable period in these two countries.

Hence I have thought it proper to arrange the Spanish scenes and pictures of costumes shown in the book in this order—Toledo and the rest of Castile, Aragon (Saragossa), Barcelona and the rest of Catalonia, and finally the sheets that deal with other landscapes, and I have preceded this arrangement only with the sheets depicting definite persons or having some relation to the imperial court, to which the representations of Indians also belong. Within these different groups the larger scenes portraying the life of the people and containing several figures have been placed ahead of the mere costume pictures.

And here, too, Weiditz showed the same keen powers of observation as in his real line of medal portraitist and recorded with sure lines everything that impressed him as especially worth while on his trips through the country or in the cities. Thus he shows us the Spanish peasant at his plough (plates XXIX, XXX) and at the work of threshing his corn, which was done by using a threshing cradle (plates XXXI, XXXII), winnowing (plate XXXIII), and transporting the grain (plate XXXIV). His attention is equally drawn to the custom of keeping wine in goatskins (plates XXV, XXVI, XLVII), as to the well organised and for Spain so important watersupply (plates XXXV, XXXVI; LXIII, LXIV; LXXIV). In another place one sees plainly what a strong impression was made on him by the municipal and rural police, "which is worthy of all honour." This police body, which had grown up out of the "holy Hermandad," was what is today called the "Guardia civil" (plates XXXVII—XLV), and one notes also the horror aroused in him by the public flagging of illdoers, of a pickpocket (plate XL) or of the old woman evidently suspected of being a witch (plates XLIII—XLV), though criminals were no more gently treated in Germany at that time, indeed, quite the opposite.

The beggars for ransom money must at that time have constituted an especially striking type in the streets of Spain. These were persons who had been taken prisoner by Chaireddin Barbarossa, but who had escaped and now travelled about the country begging for funds to pay the ransom of their friends who were still in captivity (plate XLVI). Not until later years (1532/33) did Andreas Doria, upon command of the Emperor, begin the battle against the pirates, who were becoming steadily more insolent and daring and had recently made an alliance with Turkey. Through daring expeditions and feats of endurance the Mediterranean was gradually cleansed of them.

In the populous and busy Barcelona Weiditz was attracted especially by the life and operations in the harbour, by the manner in which the ships there were drawn "up and down" (plate LX), the horses brought on board of ships (plate LXII), skiffs repaired (plate LXIII), galley slaves used for all kinds of labour (plates LXV, LXVI), women water carriers in Catalonia bearing incredible burdens on their heads (plate LXXIV), etc. Here for the first time he seems to have seen the "crab without pincers," that is to say, a languste, and a tame weasel (plate LXXIII).

And in the same manner in which he gave particular representation of details of daily life that impressed him as noteworthy, and added them to his pictures as a supplement, in like manner one finds in the costume pictures, which form the overwhelming majority in his costume-book, now and then also special treatment of certain original details, such as the peculiar cape of the miller's apprentice (plate XXXIV) or the "Spanish apron" (plate LXIII). These things, together with the zeal with which he endeavoured as far as possible to unite in his work representatives from all classes of the people, give the plainest evidence of the interest in the history of costumes—an interest that seems almost modern—that must have characterised Christoph Weiditz.

We make the acquaintance also of certain personages. In addition to Ferdinand Cortez (plate IX), we find above all Andreas Doria in the deliberately modest dress which furnished such a contrast to the Emperor and the imperial splendour at Barcelona (plate V), as well as the rich heiress Doña Menzia Zenette of the house of Mendoza, who had become the wife of Count Heinrich of Nassau (plate VII), and in addition to these, apart from the artist himself (plate I), the owner, captain and pilot of the ship upon which Christoph Weiditz then, after the proud flotilla had started out to sea, in all probability followed the entourage of the Emperor (plates II, III and VI). The artist probably made the journey to Spain by the land route, from Augsburg by way of Ulm, Zurich, Geneva, Lyon, Albi, Toulouse, and from there to the coast of Roussillon, at that time still a Spanish possession, but, as has been already said, no certain details regarding the course of the trip can be found.

But certain other costume pictures also, in particular the one of the elegant Spanish lady whom he pictured with great detail from both rear and side view (plates XLVIII, XLIX), appear to point to his intercourse with the court, or, more properly speaking to the intercourse of his patron Johannes Dantiscus, though it is true that the great majority of the costume pictures from Spain give the impression that he also noted them on his walks through the streets of the city or on his tramps through the country, and quickly sketched them. It is particularly true of the larger scenes, such as the horseback ride of the Prelate of Toledo (plates XXVII, XXVIII), the horseback ride of the married couple in Valladolid, with their servant running along behind (plate LXXVIII), the entourage of the mourning noblewoman of Catalonia (plates LXXIII, LXXIV), the Catalonian couple travelling across the country (plates LXXV, LXXVI), or the horseback ride of the "citizens" in Valencia (plate LXXVIII), which city Weiditz apparently became acquainted with. The same can also be said of many individual figures, among which I incline especially to include the Spanish nobleman on horseback (plate LI)—provided that this figure does not represent one of the Alguazil who were regarded by our artist with timid reverence—, the Castilian peasant (plate LII), the Castilian shepherd (plate LV), the negro slave (plate XLII), as well as the two penitents (plates LVI, LVII). For we can assume that the processions of Spanish flagellants, if he encountered them, made an indelible impression on our good Augsburger.

With very few exceptions, to which the two last named plates belong, all of the representations thus far mentioned do not, as far as we know, possess any counterpart either in the elder or in the later literature and art. Hence we have good reason to regard this whole series of pictures as the result of Weiditz's Spanish trip and as his own conception and work. However, continuing for a moment our consideration of Spain, the case is different as to the three larger groups of costume pictures and scenes, the most of which we encounter again in later works, mainly with greater or less differences, but often the same in all details. This is particularly the case in the so called Heldt costume-book, that is, the extraordinarily comprehensive codex which Sigmund Hagelsheimer, known by the name of Heldt, had caused to be collected in Nuremberg about the middle of the 16th century and which is still preserved today in the costume library of Baron von Lipperheide in the state art library in Berlin.[11]

In the second part of this introduction an exact page for page comparison is made between this Heldt costume-book and our manuscript. This shows us that Christoph Weiditz as a rule, in the text as well as in the pictures of these three groups, offers us the more primitive, that is to say, that he stood nearer than Heldt to the prototype which can be imagined to have existed for certain parts of the manuscript.

---

[11] A detailed description of the contents of the Heldt costume-book will be found in the catalogue of the Lipperheide costume library, first volume (Berlin 1896—1901) page 5 et seq. under No. 4. On certain pages of the volume one finds the dates 1548, 1550, 1560, 1564, 1565, etc., up to 1581. The publishers of the catalogue, however, believed that these figures relate only in part to the years in which the costume-book was made, and they ascribe the origin of the book, which in any case required many years, to the period from 1560 to 1580.

Among these are the representations of the Indians (plates XI—XXIII). With the exception of the first picture (plates XI, XII) which shows the Indians at a game of throwing and catching, and the last sheet of our series (plate XXIII), all these pictures have their counterpart, though in part spoiled, in the Heldt book also.   The text accompanying the first scene contains a reference to Ferdinand Cortez, who had brought these Indians to His Imperial Majesty "from India," which inclines me to believe that Weiditz himself had an opportunity to observe these wild people in their activities and games at the court of the Emperor, whose lively interest in and care for the Indians are often apparent, and that he then pictured them.   So it is possible that this group of pictures belonged to the original works of our artist, and that they then, either in the form in which we have them or in the assumed original and more sketched execution, might have formed directly or indirectly the patterns for Sigmund Heldt.   For it goes without saying that Heldt, when he made the plans for his comprehensive costume-book, reached out feelers in all directions.   This is shown, among other things, by the close relation of Heldt to the great Frankfort publisher Sigmund Feyerabend.   Unfortunately we know nothing whatever about the earlier history of the Weiditz costume-book.   It is possible that his precise work was very well known in interested circles, and it is very probable that the sheets were sold shortly after his death in 1559.

I can hardly regard the peculiarly armed soldier whom I have placed at the end of this series (plate XXIII) as an original work of Christoph Weiditz.   On the contrary, I assume that the figure was probably taken from one of the earlier woodcuts whose numbers increased rapidly following the first appearance of the Vespucci letter (1503), which was shortly followed by many editions in the most various languages.[12]   Indeed, the whole form of the face and treatment of the hair make it appear doubtful whether we actually have here an Indian instead of a Malay or a man from the Indies, whose picture Weiditz may have run across on one of his trips or in Augsburg, and then, mistaking the wealthy Golconda for a part of America, fitted him out with a dress of parrot feathers for use in his costume-book.

A similar connection is also found in the second series of pictures between the Weiditz costume-book and the Heldt manuscript, namely in the detailed representation of the Moriscos, their house and street costumes, and their home and social life.   These sheets (plates LXXIX to XCI) also appear, with only one questionable exception (cf. note to plate LXXXIII) in Heldt's book. The Weiditz texts give nearly everywhere a more intimate and original impression (cf. e. g. plate LXXXV), while the pictures offered by Heldt appear to be closer in some respects to the prototype which we can perhaps assume.

At the time of Christoph Weiditz' Spanish trip the Moriscos had preserved their old costumes and usages virtually only in Granada, but even there the women had long since been compelled to abandon the traditional face covering worn on the streets and had substituted for it a broad mantle, with which it was possible for them to cover their faces almost entirely.   This, especially for the foreigner, striking appearance of the Morisco woman in her street costume has left numerous traces in the costume pictures of the 16th century and later.   As early as the time of Ferdinand and Isabella the Moriscos, who refused to be converted to Christianity, had been treated with severe repressive measures, and around the year 1530 it was only in Granada that such a deep insight could be gained into the life of these last remnants of the old Moorish population, such as is documented both in the Weiditz and the Heldt costume-book.

---

[12] The earliest publications regarding America are listed by Henry Harisse: "A description of works relating to America published between the years 1492 and 1551," New York, 1866. In addition to this a volume "Additions," Paris, 1872. In this the pictures are also briefly referred to in part. Cf. also Rudolf Schiller, "Die älteste bekannte Abbildung südamerikanischer Indianer" in Dr. A. Petermann's reports from Justus Perthes' geographic institution, volume 71, Nos. 1 and 2 (January, 1925), page 21 et seq., and the older literature there referred to.

At best, however, it is doubtful whether Weiditz actually visited this province and was able to make his investigations and his sketches there, although he actually, as for example in the costuming of his Morisco women with an undergarment resembling a vest (cf. plates LXXX and LXXXI), undoubtedly comes closer to reality than does Heldt. I am inclined here to assume that both men, Weiditz and Heldt, independently of each other, drew their material from the same source, which is concealed from us today but perhaps was easily available in those days, or in any event, if Heldt was also dependent on Weiditz, the latter's representations were not based upon studies of the subjects, but upon an older and possibly Spanish pattern.

The same is true of the third group, which remains to be mentioned—the types from Navarre and the Basque provinces—whom we see in the long tiresome series (plates XCIX— CXXI), and whom we also find in Heldt's book with only a single and undoubtedly accidental exception (plate CXVIII). Here, too, now Weiditz and now Heldt seems to offer the more original and more dependable text and representation, and here, too, it is not at all impossible that our costume-book must be regarded as the prototype and the starting point for many later reproductions. And here again there is more evidence that these pictures were not directly made from the subjects, but that they were taken from some unknown literary and artistic predecessor. It is to be hoped that the publication of the Weiditz costume-book may shortly be followed by the discovery of these sources, from which it is to be hoped that they would throw light on so many questions and riddles, the solution of which was not possible here.

As we follow the further voyages of our artist it is to be noted first of all that Habich, basing his opinion on the medals, especially the earliest ones, which represent Christoph Mülich, who at that time (1529) lived in Italy, as well as on the undated medals depicting Johann Albert von Widmannstätter, together with their Italianising style, is inclined to assume a lengthy stay of the artist in Italy.[18] One is safe in ascribing the latter to the last part of 1529 or the beginning of 1530, at which time most of the few actual Italian costume pictures contained in our codex (plates CXLIV— CXLIX), and which have no real counterpart, with the possible exception of plate CXLV, in the Heldt manuscript, probably came into existence. Judging by these, Weiditz appears to have joined again the advance of the Emperor over the Alps in the spring of 1530, together with the Bishop of Kulm, to have returned with the Imperial entourage to Augsburg, and then, as Habich says, toward the end of the year again to have followed the Emperor to the Netherlands once more with Johannes Danticus, as the court portraitist of the Bishop. Not only the medals describe this route and this stay, but ten sheets of the costume-book (plates CXXXI—CXL) also point in the same direction. With only one exception (plate CXXXVI), these pictures have no counterpart in the Heldt codex, and in all probability they are the result of direct observation and of lively and intelligent interest in the peculiarities of the costumes in Hennegau, Holland, Seeland, Friesland, etc., and also in the customs and manners of life there. The splendid picture showing the girls in Seeland kneading bread (plate CXXXIV), or the other one showing a young woman in Hennegau who is obviously making lace (cf. the comments on plate CXXXIII), make one regret that the artist did not hand down to us from the Netherlands more extensive results of his own experiences and observations, or that, as we may again note, many other sheets may have been lost as a result of carelessness of later periods.

The two pictures of German costumes (plates CXLI and CXLII), which, as is also indicated in the text, are derived from earlier pictures, the woman of Vienna (plate CXLIII), the scanty pictures of costumes from England (plates CL and CLI), from Ireland (plate CLII), and from Portugal (plates CLIII and CLIV), were, as already noted, doubtless added only by way of comparison to complete the plan of the costume-book. And these, although no certain resemblances could thus far be found (cf. only comment on plate CLIII), were assuredly made

---

[18] Habich in the yearbook, vol. 34, pages 13—15.

in imitation of earlier pictures which Christoph Weiditz was undoubtedly able to secure for this purpose.

Only the costume pictures that have to do with the still Spanish Roussillon, including Perpignan and Narbonne, and a few French landscapes such as Languedoc, Limousin, Bretagne (plates CXXII—CXXX), show the same vital style that awakes our admiration in the case of the great majority in the artist's Spanish reminiscences. With the sole exception of the rather clumsy picture from the Bretagne (plate CXXX), the only one of this series, by the way, for which an exact although less original counterpart can be found in the costume-book of Sigmund Heldt, these had their genesis at least in part (Roussillon) in the country itself, possibly while Christoph Weiditz was travelling through the country to Spain, the life of whose people he then depicted capably and faithfully, with the whole devotion of his artistic heart and with German thoroughness, in a manner not achieved for centuries by any other artist.

Medal of Ferdinand Cortez
by Christoph Weiditz

SECOND PART
PLATES AND INSCRIPTIONS

In the following consideration of the leaves of the Christoph Weiditz costume-book the text accompanying each plate is faithfully reproduced*. The figures in parenthesis in the different sheets refer to the present confused order of the codex.

An exact description of the colours used is then given, followed by a short reference to the connection of the respective picture or figure to contemporary or later costume pictures or memorials, above all to the Heldt costume-book, coming down nearly to the end of the 16th century. However, lack of space has made it impossible to go into these developments thoroughly. For the same reason the older literature dealing with these subjects—travel descriptions, etc.—has been referred to only here and there by way of illustration.

Plate I (sheet 78) Christoph Weiditz in his sailor's dress

"Thus Stoffell weyditz voyaged over the sea with Kolman Holmschmidt."

Earth[14] green with a yellowish cast; footwear,[15] sword, hood, cape, grayish black; cross-guard of sword steel-coloured; gloves and feather white; breeches and blouse light brownish yellow with red stripes.

No counterpart.[16] The big sword which he holds in front of him so carefully has its precise counterpart in the "Memmorjbuch der Klaytung," etc., of Paul Hector Mair (Hs. 228, 2° of the Augsburg Municipal Library) as the chief weapon of the "Provisioner," etc. Cf. sheets 3a, 8a, 18a, 19b, 22a. It is worn on a grayish black belt buckled around the body.

Plate II (sheet 85) The Patron (Captain) of the ship

"This is the patron on the ship who directs and governs the ship; stands still and watches what kind of wind the ship wants; when he whistles with his whistle the members of the crew know what they have to do, and if they fail to do it he draws his whip and gives them sharp blows."

---

* These original inscriptions are written in the old "New High German," which bears much the same relation to modern high German as does the English of Chaucer to modern English. The unique flavour of Weiditz's German is naturally therefore lost in translation.—*The Translator*.

[14] The same in all pictures.

[15] The same throughout the whole book unless otherwise indicated.

[16] This means here as throughout that I have thus far not been able to find the same picture either in literature or other graphic sheets or memorials.

Colours in the main like those of plate I, except that the three rings of the otherwise black whip, the band on which the bone pipe is carried and the pipe itself are gold embossed, and that the costume shows red stripes intersected by gray ones.

No counterpart.

Plate III (sheet 86) The Pilot of the ship

"This is also an important man on a ship, who moves the rudder at the rear."

Shoes, fur collar and cap grayish black; feather white; mantle and breeches as on plate II.

No counterpart.

Plate IV (sheet 77) Ferdinand Cortez (1529)

"Don Fernando Cordesyus, 1529, at the age of 42; this man won all India for his Imperial Majesty Charles the Fifth."

The whole costume grayish black, only the hilt and cross-guard of the sword white; the Cortez coat-of-arms (cf. appendix) is borne on rose-coloured ribbons.

No counterpart, except that the breast portrait of Ferdinand Cortez is found in precisely similar form on the Weiditz medal (yearbook of the Prussian Art Collections, vol. XXXIV, plate IV, No. 7; cf. our illustration on page 24). The reverse of the medal shows a hand reaching into the clouds, under it a radiance and the inscription "Iudicium domini apprehendit eos et fortitudo eius corroboravit brachium meum." Since Cortez was born in 1485 the statement of his age in the year 1529 is not exact. The last part of the sentence appears to have reference to the later discoveries, especially those in California (1533—1535) of the great conqueror, who had returned in 1528 to Spain, but as a result of strong hostile opposition had not been able to regain his former influence, or else we have here, as often in chronology, an historical error. Furthermore the illustration corresponds well with the description which Prescott has given us of Ferdinand Cortez's outward appearance. The full length painting in the Hospital de la Purisima Concepcion in Mexico presents him standing by a table, at a much more advanced age. Cf. Carderera, Iconografía, plate LXXII (Lithograph) reproduced also by Arthur Schurig, The Conquest of Mexico by Ferdinand Cortez (Leipzig, Inselverlag, 1918), etc.

Plates V and VI (sheets 83, 84) Andreas Doria (1529). — The owner of a Spanish ship

"Andreas Doria, a Prince of Melsein (Melfi), has in His Imperial Majesty's services done many splendid deeds and is still doing them on the sea."

"Thus the owner of the ship sits on a railing on a ship in Spain when they voyage across the sea."

Doria entirely in black, with white beard and hair; the owner of the ship with black shoes, red stockings, olive-coloured breeches with gray stripes, black coat and cap, under which is a red hood, gray gold embossed dagger; sitting on a yellow railing in front of a black skiff.

No counterpart for either plate. — Doria (1466—1560) was presented by Charles V with the principality of Melfi and the overlordship of Tursis, after he had deserted Francis I of France and gone over to the Emperor. The reference to the splendid deeds obviously refers to his naval victory over the Turks (1532) and to his operations against the pirate king Chaireddin Barbarossa.

Plates VII and VIII (sheets 35, 36) Imperial baggage waggon in Castile

"Waggons and drivers of this kind are used in Castile when His Imperial Majesty has baggage loaded for a trip across the country."

Waggon yellowish brown with steel-coloured, silver embossed nails on the hub of the wheel; covering bordered with lilac, with black eagle with gold aureole about the head; the left mule white, the right one grayish brown; the driver with blue blouse, green hood and yellowish cap.

No counterpart in any literature thus far known.

Plate IX (sheet 59) Doña Menzia Zenette of the house of Mendoza

"This is the Margravine von Zenette, wife of Count Heinrich von Nassau; in this manner they go about in the kingdom of Toledo; thus she looks after her lord as he travels with His Imperial Majesty over the sea to Genua."

Violet red dress with olive-coloured, gold embossed facings on the sleeves; puffs of the sleeves white, with greenish gold embossed rings and gold lacings. Head dress and shirt white, gold embossed; boat brownish black.

No counterpart. The person pictured is the third wife of Count Heinrich III of Nassau-Breda (born 1483, ruled 1516—1538), who married her in 1524 and thus became the owner of extensive estates in Spain. Such holdings, especially the castle Calahorra on the Almeria eastward from Granada, are occasionally mentioned by Dr. Johannes Lange, court physician of Friedrich II of the Palatinate, in his diary covering the trip to Spain to the Imperial camp at Granada, which he undertook in 1526 in the retinue of his master. Cf. Adolf Hasenclever's publication in the archive for cultural history, vol. 5, (1907), pages 414, 415 and 423.

Plate X (sheet 66) Army drummer by the entry of the Emperor

"Thus ride the army drummers in Spain when the Emperor rides into a city."

The negro youth in white, silver embossed upper garment and reddish violet, gold embossed undergarment; earring golden, cap blue, feather white, the drums brown and yellow, gold embossed, with white, silver embossed drumheads; small covering red, gold embossed; big covering violet, gray, green and yellow striped. Mule brown with gray hoofs and black bridle, trimmed with gold at the mouth.

No counterpart.

Plates XI and XII (sheets 12, 13) Indians playing Mora and catch-stone

"These are Indian people whom Ferdinand Cortez brought to His Imperial Majesty from India and they have played before His Imperial Majesty with wood and ball" (cf. the following plates).
"With their fingers they gamble like the Italians."

Skins grayish brown, hair black; lilac coloured leather breeches with white, gold embossed seams; earrings and bracelets white, gold embossed; stones, including those in the faces, red, white and blue, in part gold embossed.

Both of these plates, which show the Indians at their games with stones and the Mora game (Italian Morra, French Mourre), have no counterpart. As to the different games of catch played with stones, wooden balls, etc., cf. Zeitschrift des Vereins für Volkskunde XVI (1906) page 46 et seq., XVII (1907) page 85 et seq., 89 et seq., 91 et seq., XXVIII (1918) page 26 et seq.

Plates XIII and XIV (sheets 10, 11) Indians playing ball

"In such manner the Indians play with the blown-up ball with the seat without moving their hands from the ground; they have also a hard leather before their seat in order that it shall receive the blow from the ball, they have also such leather gloves on."

The same colours as in plates 11 and 12; the hand-leather and the ball, like the leather breeches, light violet.

Cf. Heldt, sheets 372b–373a, with completely damaged text (cf. the German version). Weiditz's illustrations are incomparably more artistic; in the Heldt illustrations a suggestion of turf and herbs.

Plate XV (sheet 8) Indian Performance with a wooden block (1. phase)

"This is an Indian, he lies on his back and throws a block of wood around on his heels, is as long as a man and as heavy, he has on the earth a leather under him, is as big as a calf skin."

Colour of hair and skin here and on the following plates the same as on the plates XI—XIV; apron grayish black; feathers on the feet red, blue, green and white, and also the in part gold embossed girdle; the borders of the leather lying on the earth lilac, the block of wood yellowish.

Cf. Heldt, sheet 374a, where this blanket under the Indian plainly appears as reddish leather. Otherwise, however, Weiditz's text and illustration (Heldt does not show the feathers on the feet) are closer to the assumed common prototype.

Plate XVI (sheet 6) Indian Performance with a wooden block (2. phase)

"Thus he throws the wood above him with the feet."

Same colours as on plate XV, except that there is no green on the girdle.

Cf. Heldt 375b with text, which most properly belongs to sheet 374b (Weiditz plate XVII). The inscriptions have been exchanged here.

Plate XVII (sheet 9) Indian Performance with a wooden block (3. phase)

"Thus he again catches the wood on his feet as he has thrown it up."

Same colours as on plate XV.

Cf. Heldt 374b, but with the inscription belonging to sheet 375b; see the preceding number. See also in the artistically excellent costume-book of 1580 in the Lipperheide collection (catalogue No. 13), page 30: "Arabian Moor playing with a block," and on page 31: "how an Arabian Moor plays with a block." Both Weiditz and Heldt, however, characterise the players more plainly as Indians by wiry hair, by stones inserted in the skin, etc.

Plate XVIII (sheet 1) Indian woman

"In this manner the Indian women go. Not more than one of them has come out" (that is, to Europe).

Upper garment light gray with yellow, gold embossed border; lower part green with red border; headdress green, red and white; necklace golden with red ornament.

Cf. Heldt, sheet 370b. — Weiditz's text is nearer the original. In some respects Heldt's illustration is nearer to the original and in some respects that of Weiditz. Thus Heldt's Indians have a blue and red "beauty plaster" on the cheek, a white one on the forehead and a wilder expression of the face, while Weiditz indicates feathers, which are entirely lacking in Heldt's picture, and the hair of Heldt's Indians is long and in ringlets. Cf. also H. Weigel and Jost Amann, Habitus praecipuorum populorum (Nuremberg 1577), sheet CLXXXIII, which may have been derived from Heldt.

Plate XIX (sheet 2) Indian man

"Thus the Indians go, have costly jewels let into their face, can take them out when they want to and can put them in again." Supplementary: "wooden bowl."

Mantle light gray and green striped with yellow, gold embossed border; feather apron reddish and pale gray; girdle red, green, blue and white; bowl white, gold embossed.

Cf. Heldt, 371a ("the manner in which the Indian men go"), but Weiditz's text and illustration (feathers) are nearer to the original. Stones in the face are also shown in the case of Indians from Brazil, etc., by Weigel and Amann (1577), sheets CLXXXI—CLXXXII. — The custom of the Indians, so striking to the European, of "decorating" their faces by inserting stones, bones, etc., is referred to in the earliest literature. Thus one finds in the letter which Amerigo Vespucci, probably in the spring of 1503, sent to his Florentine fellow countryman Lorenzo Pietro de Medici: "They carry seven stones in their lips, many of which are as long as a half shoe," and in the later editions of the letter: "The men are accostumed to bore holes in their lips and cheeks and they then stick bones and stones into these holes, and you are not to believe that these are very small ones." In the letter written by Giovanni di Lionardi da Empoli on September 16, 1504, from Lisbon to his father to Florence, one reads: "They ornament themselves with parrot feathers and they stick fish bones in the lips." In a woodcut from the same period, which was doubtless based on the Vespucci letter, one reads: "The men have also many precious stones in their faces and breasts." Cf. Rudolf Schuller (Petermanns Mitteilungen, 71. year, 1925, page 21 et seq.).

Plate XX (sheet 3) Another Indian

"This is also an Indian man."

Mantle red and striped with dirty blue, inside green; feather apron reddish and light gray; girdle white, red and bluish; necklace white, gold embossed.

Cf. Heldt, sheet 371b, in which, however, the feather apron is lacking and the whole illustration is more summarily treated. Weiditz's text is also the older.

Plate XXI (sheet 5) Indian with a wooden drinking jug

"This is also the Indian manner, how they have brought wood jugs with them out of which they drink."

Blanket red and yellow (gold embossed), with grayish blue border; jug white with gold and red stripes, bluish gray foot and handle; necklace white, gold embossed, with red stones; earring golden with green stone.

Cf. Heldt, sheet 370a. Weiditz's text older and illustration more detailed, but turf and herbs are slightly indicated by Heldt.

Plate XXII (sheet 4) Indian chief ("Noble")

"This is also an Indian, a nobleman of their kind."

Apron white, green, red and grayish blue, the feathers rose and gray; sunshade also red, white, green, and grayish blue, the middle star yellowish (gold embossed), with grayish blue centre point; parrot green and rose, with gray beak and claws; laurel twig olive green with white berries; neck-cord red.

Cf. Heldt, sheet 372a, where, however, parrot and twig are missing and the man stands on turf upon a fourcornered oblong stone plate. All details very coarsely painted without reproducing the feathers, etc. Weiditz's text is also older. The parrot may have been taken from Hans Burgkmair's woodcut representing wild people, the only existing copy of which is in the possession of Baron Ludwig von Welser in Neunhof near Lauf, and a photograph thereof in the copper engraving cabinet of the Germanic Museum, or it may have been taken from the copy of this picture published by Balthasar Sprenger, which shows in addition to Burgkmair's two parrots a third one very badly drawn.

Plate XXIII (sheet 7) Indian (?) with his accoutrement

"Thus they go in India with their arms two thousand miles away, where gold is found in the water."

Loincloth white, green, red and grayish blue; feathers grayish brown; neck ornaments golden, with bluish gray, red and white feathers; the toothed edge of the weapon steel-coloured, the shaft yellowish, the middle part grayish white and golden between white (gold embossed) and red tassels; the shield with grayish blue cross, the oval bordered with green, the whole surrounded by gray fur.

No direct counterpart. This seems not to be an Indian, but a man from the Indies, who was confused with the former. The Sprenger copy of the Burgkmair woodcut referred to under the foregoing plate may have been one of the first ones for illustrations of this kind.

Plate XXIV (sheet 17) Dress of a rich prelate in Toledo

"Thus the rich prelates go in the kingdom of Toledo."

Prelate dressed entirely in black, but with grayish white gloves and a gold buckle on the hat; the boy (with light brown hair) in white, silver embossed blouse and red trousers.

Cf. Heldt, sheet 256 a ("a Spanish priest"), where the hat is pulled far down over the face and badly drawn. Heldt's prelate wears no cap under his hat and no gloves. Hence Weiditz's text and representation are undoubtedly older. See also Bertelli (Venice 1563), sheet 50 ("Sacerdos Hispanus"), but Weiditz is much more exact. Weigel and Amann (1577), sheet CLIV, also evidently misrepresented.

Plates XXV and XXVI (sheets 33, 34) Transporting wine in Toledo

"In this manner wine is carried in Toledo in goatskins."

Waggonbox and goatskins reddish violet, the other part of the waggon yellowish, left horse yellowish, the right dark brown; coverings and neck ornaments grayish white; the driver in gray, silver embossed mantle and hood; the undergarment with blue sleeves, gray whip with yellowish handle.

No counterpart. Both literature and art frequently refer to wine in goatskins and to the hides used for this purpose ("bota"), which Don Quixote mistook for giants. (See the diary of Dr. Johannes Lange covering his voyage from Beilngries to Granada in 1526; Archiv für Kulturgeschichte V, 1907, page 432). See also the engraving by Georg Hufnagel (1564), Braun und Hogenberg, Beschreibung und Contrafactur von den vornembsten Stetten der Welt, vol. V, on the first picture of "Zahara."

Plates XXVII and XXVIII (sheets 45, 46) Toledan prelate riding

"In this manner the Spanish prelates go riding in Toledo, with a youth running behind them, who trots along in slippers."

Prelate dressed entirely in black, mule dark reddish brown, with black, gold ornamented bridle, the stirrups steel-coloured; the boy (with blond hair) in red, silver embossed jacket and with trousers probably originally white, but now covered with reddish spots which conceal the original colour.
No counterpart.

Plates XXIX and XXX (sheets 55 and 56) Spanish peasant ploughing

"Thus they till in Spain."   To this an unintelligible supplement.

Ploughman's cap crimson red, silver embossed; jacket blue; apron grayish white, silver embossed; breeches red, gold embossed; right ox yellowish brown, the left brownish black; hoofs and horns light gray; cutting edge and point of instrument in the ploughman's right hand steel-coloured; handles, plough and yoke yellowish; the soil dark gray, with a green stripe of meadow at the horizon.
No counterpart. The ploughman on the G. Hufnagel engraving "Granata" of 1565 published by Braun and Hogenberg, vol. V, also has the same kind of peculiar instrument in his right hand. It was undoubtedly used for breaking up the clods.

Plates XXXI and XXXII (sheets 37, 38) Threshing corn in Spain

"In this manner they thresh corn in Spain, they draw a board back and forth across it on which stones are laid."

The peasant in white hat, white, silver embossed blouse (with grayish blue cuffs) and breeches; red, silver embossed stockings; left horse light brown with grayish-white neck decoration, the right horse gray, the bridle grayish black; yoke, whip, threshing board and corn yellowish, and dirty brown in the shaded parts.
No counterpart, but this ancient Spanish method of threshing with the threshing board or cradle has been referred to at different times, described and also pictured. Johannes Lange, already referred to (page 415), notes in 1526 how the Spaniards "do not thresh the grain, but have asses, oxen and horses walk across it, drawing a board full of sharp stones fitted into it, and thus tread out the grain so that the straw is chopped to about a finger's length wherefore the horses and cattle have no straw." Cervantes also makes a similar report in Don Quixote. "The threshing floors 'las eras' (from the Latin area) lie outside of the village. They are roomy places, the ground of which consists of clay trodden hard. The grain is thrown on to them and then threshed with the threshing cradle, which is drawn by horses, who are driven by the person standing there, kept going around until all the corn is threshed out" (Adolf Schulten, "Spain in the Don Quixote of Cervantes," in Spanien, Zeitschrift für Auslandskunde, year 1919, vol. 2, page 103). This process is repeatedly pictured in the 16th century (1574, for instance). See Braun and Hogenberg, vol. I, view of "Vallisoletum" (Valladolid), and the representation of "Orchuna" (Osuna) in vol. IV.

Plate XXXIII (sheet 40) Cleaning corn in Spain

"Thus they cleanse the grain in Spain."

Hood white, silver embossed; jacket red, gold embossed; coat blue; sandals yellowish with black stripes; sieve yellowish.

Cf. Heldt, sheet 352b ("Thus the miller woman goes in Spain"). Weiditz's text appears older, but Heldt is nearer the original in his colouring—jacket e. g. grayish blue, with white, out-turned cuffs.

Plate XXXIV (sheet 39) Transporting corn and flour in Spain

"In this manner they carry the sack of flour on asses to the mill in Spain."

Hood with visor grayish white, silver embossed; blouse green with black girdle; breeches light blue, sack light gray, ass light brown, with light gray hoofs.

No counterpart. Similar pictures—the ass in the favorite animal of the Spanish peasant (cf. Schulten, page 93)—abound in the 16th century. See e. g. Braun and Hogenberg, vol. 5, "Palacios."

Plates XXXV and XXXVI (sheets 41, 42) Castilian waterseller

"Thus they bring water in Castile in many big cities to sell it on the streets."

Hood green, silver embossed; blouse red, silver embossed; breeches grayish white, silver embossed; stockings blue, stick yellowish; saddle bluish, silver embossed; bridle green, in part black, in part silver trimmings; baskets yellowish brown, vessels reddish, mule grayish white with gray hoofs.

No counterpart. Braun and Hogenberg 1, 5 ("Granada") and V, 8 in the picture of the small mountain city "Jerenna" show a similar transport with somewhat different packsaddle.

Plate XXXVII (sheet 31) Spanish bailiff

"Here the Spanish bailiff is going along."

Cap carmine with green rim, blouse grayish black; sleeves of undergarment light yellow; hanging sleeves green, silver embossed; breeches red; shield, cross-guard of sword and lower end of lance steel-coloured, lance shaft yellowish, sword gray.

No counterpart.

Plate XXXVIII (sheet 32) Spanish police officer ("Alguacil")

"Here the Spanish policeman is riding along. God knows how pious they are! This is the red staff that one had better not get acquainted with."

Cap black with gold button, mantle green, blouse bluish, sleeves and breeches crimson, boots yellowish, silver embossed; stick yellowish, sword black, cross-guard and basket hilt golden, stirrups and spurs steel-coloured; horse light gray with gray hoofs; bridle green with golden ornamentation, grayish blue tassel and crimson fringes.

No counterpart. The "alguacil" is today a court or police attendant.

Plate XXXIX (sheet 29) Spanish court-usher

"This here is a preganther or crier in Castile, who goes ahead and cries when an evildoer is punished."

Cap gray, hooded mantle blue; the cloth on the shoulder red, silver embossed; breeches dirty lilac colour, instrument dark grey with gold trimmings.

No counterpart. The public crier in Spain is today called "pregonero", and "preguntador" means questioner.

Plate XL (sheet 30) Punishing a cut-purse in Spain

"These are the pious Spaniards who cut off pockets or otherwise steal them, one beats them in this manner on an ass."

Supplementary inscription gives the German and Spanish word for "thief" and the German name for "hangman."

"Hangman's" cap grayish, blouse red, silver embossed; breeches bluish, legs naked, instrument grayish black; thief's cap gray with white facing; upper apron (shirt?) white, lower one blue; saddle gray in front and with yellowish border, yellowish at the rear with gray border; mule reddish brown; bridle gray with round blue insertion.

No counterpart.

Plate XLI (sheet 63) Another Spanish policeman

"This is also a policeman, one of the pious lads who deserve all honour."

Cap black with golden button, mantle blue, blouse red, gold embossed; breeches light gray, boots red, gold embossed; spurs, stirrups, basket of sword and cross-guard steel-coloured, sword black, saddle yellowish, gold embossed, with green trimming; bridle red, gold embossed, with green, gold embossed trimming; green, gold embossed tassel and golden ornament; horse grayish white, with gray hoofs and black bellyband.

No counterpart.

Plate XLII (sheet 61) A Spanish beadle

"Thus the beadle goes about."

Cap, mantle and sword black, except for the steel-coloured cross-guard and hilt; blouse blue, breeches red, golden embossed. Hair and beard blond.

No counterpart.

Plates XLIII and XLIV (sheets 75, 76) Flogging of a Spanish female criminal

"The man leads her along in this manner on an ass and beats her with a whip."

Executioner's cap black, jacket blue, vest and breeches red, silver embossed, dark brown beard; whip as on the preceding plate. The woman with gray hair, dressed as on the preceding plate, except that the undergarment is silver embossed; ass yellowish with gray hoofs; green bridle, yellowish saddle on a black saddlecloth. The house white, with reddish bricks, green trees; the upper windows gray-violet, edged with brown; lower windows brown.

No counterpart. Cf. note to following sheet. The Braun and Hogenberg picture also obviously deals with the expulsion of several criminals who are being whipped out of town.

Plate XLV (sheet 62) Punishing a female criminal in Spain

"In this manner they beat the old women who steal, and set them on the ladder; after that they throw wool into their wounds."

Executioner's cap red, jacket green, silver embossed; undergarment blue, breeches red, gold embossed; naked legs, brownish hair and beard; whip black with yellowish stock; woman's cap white with red triangles and red tassels; grayish brown uppergarment, grayish white, silver embossed undergarment; brownish hair; ladder grayish yellow with gray shading.

No counterpart. Something remotely similar appears to be pictured in the Braun and Hogenberg picture of Sevilla V, 7, where boys on the street throw sand and stones at the half-naked woman culprit who is riding on an ass, her hands bound, and surrounded by flies and mosquitos.

Plate XLVI (sheet 21) Collector of ransom for the prisoners of pirates

"In this manner the poor people, who have been the captives of Barbar Rossa, go around begging for God's sake that their friends who are still captives may be ransomed."

Cap green with reddish-violet facing, shirt white, silver embossed; sleeves green, silver embossed; breeches yellowish, silver embossed; legs naked, hair and beard gray, silver embossed; the box for alms yellowish, the coins gray (perhaps originally silver), the certificate white, silver embossed, with dependant yellow seal.

No counterpart. See page 18 for the expeditions of the pirate king Chaireddin Barbarossa.

Plate XLVII (sheet 22) Negro slave with a wineskin in Castile

"Thus the Moors who have been sold carry wine in goatskins in Castile; if they run away from their masters, they have to work thus and wear chains."

Blouse red, silver embossed; collar, girdle and breeches white, silver embossed; legs naked, chain and foot-irons steel-coloured; goatskin white, silver embossed; kinky hair deep black, skin dark brown.

No counterpart.

Plates XLVIII and XLIX (sheets 57, 58) Dress of a Spanish noblewoman

"Thus the women in Spain look from the front and rear."

Bonnet and other head ornaments gold embossed, with golden ribbons and balls, and bluish stones (?) set in gold; golden earrings with red centre; plastron white and brownish, neck adornment golden and gray on golden ribbon; jacket violet, silver striped, with green trimmings which are held together at the sleeves by gold and crimson clasps; cuffs white with gold in the middle; bouquet-holder golden, the flowers crimson and golden; fan white, gold embossed, with violet handle and violet centre, edged with green; overskirt violet, silver striped; underskirt crimson with white stripes and black half moons; sandals white, gold embossed, with black zigzag and crimson leather.

Almost the same costume, particularly in respect of head adornment and the characteristic sleeves, is found in the picture of Princess Isabella, the eldest daughter of Ferdinand the Catholic and Isabella of Castile, who was born in 1470, married in 1490 Don Alfonso, the eldest son of the King of Portugal, soon became a widow and died in 1498. The contemporaneous painting is in the National Museum in Madrid. A picture of it can be found in Carderera's Iconographia española . . . desde el siglo XI hasta el XVII (Madrid 1855—64), vol. II, plate LXI. The parts of the costume referred to above are described as follows in the original French text: "Sa longue chevelure d'un blond-rouge est ramassée dans un reseau de soie blanche lié avec de petits cordons (in the Spanish text: "liada por condocillos azulados") . . . Les manches ne couvrent que le haut des bras; le bas laisse à decouvert la chemise où l'on a figuré des plis abondants et qui est ramassée en cinque endroits par autant de cordons, qui s'attachent à la bande-manche de la robe ou jupe." The costume is also found in other earlier and later works. Cf. also Heldt, sheet 382a ("Thus the imperial maids look in Spain at Toledo") and 383b. Weiditz's drawing is more detailed than Heldt's, who does not show any earrings, the ornamentation of the plastron, the six balls at the end of the hair braid, the halfmoon ornaments of the undergarment and the broad trimming of the jacket. But while his drawing is closer to the original, Heldt's text appears in this case to be nearer to it. Some counterparts are also found in Heldt's sheet 380b.

Plate L (sheet 23) Castilian woman going to church

"In this manner the women in the kingdom of Castile go about the streets and to the church." Supplement: "Senora."

Hat and mantle black, the former having tassels attached to white, gold embossed buttons and ornamented with a bluish stone set in gold, the uppermost tassel also surrounded by a ring of grayish white pearls; breast covering black, necklace of grayish blue beads, with a pendant consisting of grayish blue stone, set in gold and surrounded by silver embossed grayish white pearls; overgarment light green, silver embossed and gold bordered; bow at the waist violet, the rosary white, gold embossed; undergarment crimson with grayish-violet trimming; the high soles of the shoes showing alternate white and gray ornaments and gray-crimson-white triangles between gold bands. The page in red, gold embossed blouse, with violet breeches, hair blond.

Cf. Heldt, sheet 255b ("A young woman in Spain"), but both Weiditz's text and drawing are unquestionably nearer the original. In Heldt's drawing the little page, in contrast to Weiditz's drawing, is not carrying the train or rather real dress, but the white throw, which is cross-striped with red; there are no beads on the rosary. The fingers of the outstretched right hand are unnaturally spread. This figure can be found in many of the later costume-books. Thus we see it, closer to Heldt than to Weiditz, in Ferdinando Bertelli's Omnium fere gentium . . . habitus (Venice, 1563), sheet 49; in H. Weigel's (1577), plate CLX, and again, but without the page, drawn by the modern artist of the journal "Wieland," vol. 5 (1919 - 1920), No. 10, page 21.

Plate LI (sheet 47) Spanish nobleman riding

"This is a Spanish nobleman who is riding horseback."

Cap violet, silver embossed, with golden button; undergarment red at the top and green at the bottom, mantle grayish black, legs and feet red; horse yellowish brown, with violet, silver embossed, gold decorated bridle and saddle, and with gray hoofs; stirrups and spurs steel-coloured, whip green with brownish yellow stock.

No counterpart.

Plate LII (sheet 19) Castilian peasant going to market

"This is a Castilian peasant as he goes into a city to market or rides upon an ass."

Head dress and breeches grayish white, silver embossed, the former with bluish, red and white fringes; mantle, sandals and snaps on the gray shoes yellowish; the mantle with bluish, red

and white zigzag ornaments; hood with long tassellike appendix with red, silver embossed pads, green fringes, alternating with bluish, white (silver embossed), rose, white, bluish inserts; sleeves green, silver embossed.
No counterpart.

Plate LIII (sheet 26) Bewailing the dead in Castile

"Thus they mourn in the kingdom of Castile when a friend dies."

Costume entirely black, beard gray, silver embossed.
Cf. Heldt, sheet 377b. Weiditz's picture is incomparably more artistic.

Plate LIV (sheet 27) Bewailing the dead in Castile

"Thus the women in Castile wail and also violently cry out wherefore he died, for they certainly were beautiful and rich and pious."

Costumes entirely black, rosary golden.
Cf. Heldt, sheet 378a ("Thus the woman mourns in Castile"). Weiditz's text is here much nearer the original. A picture of this sort undoubtedly influenced Cesare Vecellio, Habiti antichi et moderni di tutto il Mondo (Venice, 1589), sheet 256.

Plate LV (sheet 20) Castilian shepherd

"This is a Castilian shepherd."

Hair, shoes and stick yellowish, the last with steel-coloured crook; overgarment and breeches white, silver embossed; undergarment blue, silver embossed.
No counterpart.

Plate LVI (sheet 70) Castilian penitent (Flagellant)

"In this manner the sinners in Castile do the penance imposed upon them on Maundy Thursday."

Clothing entirely grayish black, whip black, the wounds in the back blood-red.
Cf. Heldt, sheet 376, which is a precise counterpart. Heldt however has confused the inscriptions; the text of his 375b (cf. following Weiditz sheet) belongs here: "In this manner the poor sinners beat themselves on Maundy Thursday at night time to do the penance laid upon them." Cf., however, observation regarding the following picture. Plate LVI remotely recalls also Racinet's picture, Le Costume historique, plate 289: Penitent, Italy, 16th century. The same hood with a slit in the back ("le froc est ouvert dans le dos," etc.), leaden, many-tailed whip, the lashes tipped with iron; rapid walk. In the text: "Pénitent romain. Hier encore, il existait en Italie, des ordres religieux, qui par leurs statuts, obligeaient leurs adhérents à se flageller soit en public, soit en particulier . . ."

Plate LVII (sheet 28) Penitent in Saragossa

"In this manner they beat themselves in the kingdom of Saragossa to do their penance."

Head covering grayish brown, apron grayish white, silver embossed; whip steel-coloured with grayish black stock; wounds on back blood-red.
Cf. Heldt, sheet 375b, which is a precise counterpart. To this picture belongs Heldt's text from sheet 376a: "In this manner the men beat themselves in the kingdom of Saragossa to do

their penance." The beautiful handwritten costume-book of 1580 (Lipperheide No. 13) presents a similar picture of a male and female penitent with the inscription, "how the Christians in Spain flog themselves on Good Friday." The man here resembles Weiditz's drawing, sheet LVII (not LVI), and the woman corresponds to Heldt's picture, sheet 377a. This latter picture ("in this manner the common women do penance in Castile"), which shows a woman with bound eyes, holding in her right hand a stick with five keys attached to it (the lashes?), is lacking in Weiditz's work. There is also lacking Heldt's picture, sheet 376b: "This is also a penance, it is iron or some other weight, which the sinner has to carry about in Castile," where the penitent is obliged to carry a big gray, flat object. The name "Castilia," which is lacking at this place with Heldt, may have been taken by Weiditz from the prototype of Heldt's 376b and 377a for the plate LVI. As to the mention by Racinet of the appearance in Italy of the Flagellants see in regard to Spain the diary already mentioned of Johannes Lange (page 414) of the year 1526, and also Don Juan Alvarez de Colmenar, Les Délices de l'Espagne et du Portugal, VI. vol. (Leiden, 1715), page 887: "Ce jour-là toutes les Dames paroissent à leurs balcons, ornées comme le jour de leur nôces et apuyées sur de beaux et riches tapis. On voit à cette procession tous les Pénitens ou les Disciplinans de la ville, qui s'y rendent de tous côtez. Ils portent un long bonnet, couvert de toile batiste de la hauteur de trois piez et de la forme de pains de sucre, d'où pend un morceau de toile, qui tombe par devant, et leur couvre le visage. Il y en a quelques-uns qui prennent ce dévot exercice par un véritable motif de piété. Mais il y en a d'autres, qui ne le font que pour plaire à leurs maitresses; et c'est une galanterie d'une nouvelle espèce, inconnue aux autres Nations . . . Il se fustigent par régle et par mesure, avec une discipline de cordelettes, où l'on attache au bout de petites boules de cire, garnies de verre pointu. Celui qui fouette avec le plus de courage et d'adresse, est estimé le plus brave. Lors qu'ils rencontrent quelque Dame bien faite, ils savent se fouetter si adroitement, qu'ils font ruisseler leur sang jusques sur elle, et c'est un honeur dont elle ne manque pas de remercier le galant disciplinant. Et quand ils se trouvent devant la maison de leur maitresse, c'est alors qu'ils redoublent les coups avec plus de furie, et qu'ils se dechirent le dos et les épaules . . . Ceux qui prennent cet exercice, sont obligez d'y retourner tous les ans, faute de quoi ils tombent malades; et ce ne sont pas seulement de gens du peuple ou des bourgeois, qui font cela, mais aussi des personnes de la plus grande qualité. Les véritables Pénitens pratiques bien encore d'autres mortifications," etc. Alvarez illustrates the proceeding by a copper engraving ("Procession des Disciplinans").

Plate LVIII (sheet 16) Woman in mourning in Saragossa

"In this manner the women mourn together in Saragossa."

Mantle and hood violet, silver embossed; sleeves black, rosary yellowish, sandals red with golden ornaments.
No counterpart.

Plates LIX and LX (sheets 79, 80) How the ships are maneuvered in the harbour of Barcelona

"In this manner they draw ships out of and into the harbour of Barcelona."

The dress of both workmen completely white, in part silver embossed, except that the sleeves of the first and the cap of the second are blue, the blouse and lower part of the sleeves of the second red, silver embossed, and the straps of the rope black.
No counterpart.

Plate LXI (sheet 82) Caulking ships in Spain

"In this manner they caulk the ships in Spain."

Sailor's hat violet, blouse grayish white, silver embossed; breeches originally blue, shoes yellowish, caulking chisel steel-coloured, hammer grayish white, ship black.
No counterpart.

Plate LXII (sheet 81) Loading horses into ships

"In this manner one brings the horses into the ship when they are to voyage across the sea."

Horse light brown, bridle, harness and hoofs grayish black, gear yellowish with gray shadings.
No counterpart.

Plates LXIII and LXIV (sheets 73, 74) Ships taking in water in Barcelona

"In this manner they bring fresh water in Barcelona to the ships and galleys so that it may be done more rapidly when they provision the ships or otherwise need water."
Supplement: "A Spanish apron."

The negro at the left with white, silver embossed cap and jacket, blue breeches; steel-coloured anklets on white ground; negro at the right with white, silver embossed cap, red jacket, white, silver embossed breeches, steel-coloured anklets; windlass hook, pail hook, bail and hoops of pail and also water steel-coloured; well, tank and casks yellowish with gray shadings; apron at the left crimson, silver embossed.
Cf. Heldt, sheet 373b, which is, however, only a rough counterpart: "These are Moorish slaves on the sea, they have to draw and carry fresh water to the ships." Weiditz's text and more careful execution appear nearer to the original, but the stones of the well and the wood of the frame are better depicted by Heldt. The Spanish apron is lacking in Heldt's picture.

Plates LXV and LXVI (sheets 53, 54) Spanish galley slaves

"In this manner the slaves carry fresh water to the galleys."

The galley slave at the left with white, silver embossed cap, with red facing, red blouse, white, silver embossed breeches, steel-coloured anklets on yellowish ground, gold embossed; slave at the right with white-red-white, silver embossed cap, blue mantle over white, silver embossed jacket, white, silver embossed breeches, anklets like the other. Casks yellowish.
Cf. Heldt, sheet 381b: "When they want good water for the galleys in Valents, they themselves must carry it on board, that is their wine when they are on land; they are mostly Moors and evildoers." This sheet corresponds with Weiditz's LXV. Heldt probably meant to write "when they are on the sea." Weiditz omits this joke and abbreviates the text by speaking immediately of fresh water. Vecellio (1589) in his sheet 136, under the inscription "Sforzati," also depicts such a galley slave, with anklets on both feet, carrying a cask under his arm. The picture, however, shows no connection with Weiditz and Heldt.

Plates LXVII and LXVIII (sheets 71, 72) Escort of a noblewoman in Barcelona

"This is how the rich women in Barcelona or in the kingdom of Catalonia look."
Supplement: "These are the maids."

The woman with black, gold ornamented hat, black mantle, crimson, silver embossed head cloth, black mantle, crimson, silver embossed, gold-edged dress, with golden buttons; gold paternoster, white high sandals with red, gold embossed leather; the man in black hat and mantle, blue coat, crimson breeches; the maids with white, silver embossed hoods, black mantle, crimson dresses, white shoes with red, gold embossed leather.

Cf. Heldt, sheets 382b and 383a. Despite the supplementary inscription "the maids," Heldt depicts only one maid. The chief group is nearly the same, except that Heldt's woman has no hatband and her dress is cut so indecently low that the breasts protrude. The elevated hands are also badly drawn and do not represent the action. Thus Weiditz is much nearer the original. Bertelli (Venice 1563), sheet 48, "Hispanam," presents the woman in this case alone, in much the same manner, but the train is lacking, the attitude has been changed, and the whole execution is more summary.

Plate LXIX (sheet 68) Unmarried woman in Barcelona, front view

"In this manner the maidens in Barcelona go about, the majority with low-cut shoes."

Yellowish cap with golden tassel above blond hair; red necklace with gold pendant on a white shirt; grayish brown throw, silver embossed; dress with white and golden ornamental stripes; violet stockings, white, silver embossed shoes.

Cf. Heldt, sheet 379a, which is, however, a most unartistic daub. Heldt's text is also mutilated. In respect of costume see comments on Plate LXXI.

Plate LXX (sheet 69) Unmarried woman in Barcelona, rear view

"Thus the maidens in Barcelona appear from the rear view."

Head dress white, gold embossed, with golden extension right and left, red, gold embossed ribbons and golden tassel; throw black, striped with gold; dress blue.

Cf. Heldt, sheet 379b, which is much the same, except that Heldt does not show the remarkable extension of the bonnet in the vicinity of the ears. As to the costume compare also the representation of Salome on the picture "The beheading of John the Baptist" by Franc. Gallegos in the Prado in Madrid, reproduced by Max von Böhn, Spanien, page 247. Salome appears here in three different scenes with this braid, which, however, plainly does not end with the tassel, but breaks off squarely.

Plate LXXI (sheet 67) Woman's dress in Barcelona

"Thus they also look in Barcelona."

Olive-brown hood with golden stripes, red, gold embossed undergarment, with white, gold embossed ornamental stripes over a white shirt; violet, silver embossed overgarment; yellowish, gold embossed shoes; necklace of red pearls with golden pendant; golden clasp, set in white, silver embossed pearls; red paternoster with yellowish, gold embossed jewel.

Cf. Heldt, sheet 378b, but the woman here has naked legs and feet and wears black sandals; the undergarment on Weiditz's picture plainly shows a train, which hangs in the air in Heldt's picture. In the place of the half-moon decoration at the edge, Heldt has a group of yellow bell-shaped balls. The costume in this and both following pictures agrees in several points with the more elegant costume which Weiditz has depicted on plates XLVIII and XLIX. Cf. also Carderera, plates XLVIII, XLIX, LXIX, LXX, LXXI; these have been in part copied by Max von Böhn, Spanien, (Berlin, 1924), page 171 (Monument of Donna Mencia de Mendoza, consort of the Connétable Hernandez de Velasco, in the Capilla del Condestable of the Cathedral of Burgos, with similar puffed sleeves); 172 (Donna Isabel de Ribadeneyra, about 1520), and 254 (Johanna the Demented; the two last named with similar hood-shaped head covering as in Weiditz's LXIX), etc.

Plate LXXII (sheet 89) Woman of fashion going to church in Valencia

"In this manner the noblewomen go to church in Valencia when it is hot."

White, silver embossed, gold and brown-edged bonnet, grayish brown mantle, rose-violet, gold embossed dress; red, gold ornamented shoes; yellow, red and bluish fan with golden stick.

Cf. Heldt, sheet 381a, which is in the main the same, except that, as everywhere, Weiditz's execution is much more artistic.

Plates LXXIII and LXXIV (sheets 43, 44) Catalonian noblewoman in mourning and Spanish watercarriers

"In this manner one conducts the noblewomen when they mourn in Catalonia." Supplementary inscription: "Weasel."

"In this manner the maids in different parts of Spain carry water up hill on their heads." Supplementary inscription: "Crab without pincers" (langust).

The noblewoman clothed entirely in black, with projecting white edge of bonnet; man at the left with black hat and mantle, green sleeves and breeches, blue coat; man at the right with black hat and mantle, yellowish coat, blue breeches; the weasel grayish brown, neckband and chain steel-coloured; the watercarrier in yellowish jacket, with white, silver embossed, hood and head pad, yellowish water jar, brown pot, with green top; the langust white, silver embossed.

No counterpart. A similar watercarrier, going at high speed, reproduced by Braun and Hogenberg V, 8 ("Jerenna," famosus prope Hispalim locus).

Plates LXXV and LXXVI (sheets 51, 52) Catalonian married couple traversing the country

"In this manner the Catalans conduct their wives across country."

Man with light violet cap and breeches, blue, silver embossed coat, with lower part of sleeves red, yellow stick; Woman with light violet, silver embossed hat and mantle, hat decorated with two woolen tufts; saddle green with yellowish frame, mule light brown, hoofs gray, bridle and reins black.

No counterpart.

Plate LXXVII (sheet 109) Woman walking in the kingdom of Valencia

"In this manner the women of the kingdom of Valencia go walking in the streets."

White, silver embossed hat, gold trimmed, with three black tassels; light violet, silver embossed overgarment; red, gold embossed and gold-edged dress and light violet stockings.

Cf. Heldt, sheet 380 a: "In this manner the women in Valencia go walking in the streets with white hats and shoes." These, however, are black in Heldt's picture, where the hat is reddish white with three black buttons, fire-red dress, with grayish green border at the bottom; black throw, yellow and white sleeves, which, however, have green seams and are ornamented with green bows. Ruches at the hands, yellow ornaments. The dress in Heldt's picture is low cut and bordered with white at the top. In this case Heldt appears somewhat nearer the supposed original than Weiditz in respect to both text and picture.

The costume with the many bows on the strange sleeves resembles somewhat that of the "Donna Maria de Gurrea Duquesa de Villahermosa llamada la rica fembra" on the picture which her grandson, Duke Don Martin de Gurrea y Aragon, had painted of her in the second third of the sixteenth century, as Carderera (plate LXVII) believes, undoubtedly with the help of some articles of clothing preserved by the family for many years ("ropas y galas"). "Les manches de la robe," says Carderera's French version, "avec des taillades, qui laissent voir le linge intérieur, sont fort élégantes et pittoresques: elles figurent être relevées avec des rubans blancs à bouts garnis d'or et de pierreries" (latter lacking on our picture).

Plate LXXVIII (sheet 64) Citizens riding in Valencia

"In this manner the citizens in Valencia ride with their wives in their parks."

Man in violet hat and mantle, red, gold embossed breeches; the woman with white, silver embossed, gold ornamented head dress, crimson sleeves, blue mantle, yellow and reddish fan with formerly golden stick; mule brownish with black, gold ornamented bridle. Stirrup and spur also golden (colours in part badly faded and spoiled).

No counterpart.

Plate LXXIX (sheet 99) House dress worn by Morisco women in Granada

"In this manner the Morisco women dress at home in Granada."

Head cloth, jacket and trousers white, silver embossed; head cloth with red and green band; short stockings, red, gold embossed.

Cf. Heldt, sheet 354 b, which is precisely the same, except that the stockings are longer in the Weiditz picture.

Plate LXXX (sheet 100) House dress worn by Morisco women and children

"In this manner the Morisco women dress in their house with their children."

The woman with red and white head cloth under green, white and bluish band; brownish red vest, white, silver embossed jacket and trousers; white, gold embossed, short stockings; the child with white, green and golden striped mantle, edged with gold; red, silver embossed and apparently blue lined dress with golden buttons; short violet stockings.

Cf. Heldt, sheet 355 a, which is the same except that the upper part of the woman's body under the jacket is completely naked. Braun and Hogenberg II, 3 ("Alhama") have almost the same picture in the left foreground. Cf. as to plates LXXX and LXXXI also Weigel's plate CLXIV (1577).

Plate LXXXI (sheet 101) Morisco woman spinning in Granada

"In this manner the Morisco women spin in their house in Granada."

Green and white head cloth under blue and white band, brownish-black vest, white, silver embossed jacket and trousers, blue short stockings; the spindle yellowish with gray ring, distaff also yellowish with red and green cover.

Cf. Heldt, sheet 355b, again precisely the same except for the naked body under the jacket; Vecellio (1589), sheet 267b—268a ("Donzella di Granata"), which figure is derived from the representation like those of Weiditz and Heldt. As to Weigel see comment on foregoing plate.

Plate LXXXII (sheet 102) Morisco woman sweeping her house

"In this manner the Morisco women sweep their house."

Costume as in preceding picture, except that head cloth is striped in red, green and gold; broom with red-white-red broomstick and gray edging. Door yellowish, with steel-coloured handle and light gray masonry.

Cf. Heldt, sheet 357b, an exact counterpart except that here the surroundings are given in greater detail. Thus, for instance, two square windows with convex panes are in the wall of the house at the right, and under them stands a yellow wooden bench on which is a small dish with four dumplings, as well as a small fine jar. The attitude of the sweeping woman is somewhat different in the two pictures—Weiditz shows her in somewhat natural position, but Heldt almost running.

Plate LXXXIII (sheet 103) House dress of Morisco girls

"In this manner the Morisco maidens are dressed in their house."

Head cloth red, silver embossed, with white, gold ornamented band; golden neck ornament with green inlet; uppergarment half yellow and gold embossed and half blue and silver embossed, with golden buttons. Right sleeve light violet, silver embossed, with white facing; left sleeve red, silver embossed, with white facing; undergarment half red, silver embossed, half green; short stockings, brownish violet; naked feet and yellow sandals with black straps.

No counterpart (occasionally a sheet is missing from the Heldt codex, as for instance sheet 356).

Plate LXXXIV (sheet 97) Street dress of Morisco women in Granada

"The Morisco women look like this in the streets in Granada."

Band over forehead white, white mantle, silver embossed, with gray fringes; undergarment half yellow, gold embossed; half blue with golden buttons; short red stockings, silver embossed.

Cf. Heldt, sheet 353b, which is identical, except that less of the face can be seen in Weiditz's picture. This is the representation of the Morisco woman which one encounters most often in the later literature. Cf. for example Braun and Hogenberg I, 5 ("Granada"), upper left hand side; II, 3 ("Alhama"), upper right side (not exactly the same), and V, 14, left; Weigel (1577), sheet CLXIII; Bartolomeo Grassi, Dei veri ritratti degl' habiti di tutte le parti del mondo, etc. (Rome, 1585), plate 29: the fifth figure under the "Moreschi di Granada," and down as far as Kretschmar and Rohrbach, The Costumes of the Peoples (Die Trachten der Völker), second ed., 1882, plate 76, 1, where one finds also on page 274 a short description of the Morisco costume. As long ago as 1526 Johann Lange (page 421) wrote during his stay in Granada: "In like manner the half of the people of this state are white Moors, whose women and maidens all wear white trousers, and have on their head and body a white cloth, like the village shepherds with us, which reaches down to the calves, and they cover half of their face with the cloth."

Plate LXXXV (sheet 98) Street dress of fashionable Morisco women in Granada

"In this manner the noblewomen go about the streets in Granada" (follows an obscure name, cf. the German version).

Same colours as in the preceding plate, except that undergarment has golden seams and the stockings are grayish violet.

Cf. Heldt, sheet 354a: "A Moorish noblewoman, as she appears in the street," which is precisely the same. Weiditz's inscription, which is with difficulty understandable, is undoubtedly closer to the original than Heldt. Cf. further Braun and Hogenberg I, 5 ("Granada"), foreground, centre, etc.

Plate LXXXVI (sheet 96) Street dress of Morisco women and girls in Granada

"This shows how Morisco women and maidens look from a rear view in the kingdom of Granada."

Mantle white, silver embossed; undergarment half light green, silver embossed, half red, gold embossed; stockings blue.

Cf. Heldt, sheet 353a, which is the same, except that in Weiditz's picture the parallel folds of the mantle from top to bottom are more sharply emphasised. Cf. also Braun and Hogenberg I, 5 ("Granada"), left foreground; II, 3 ("Alhama"), left foreground; V, 14 (pose somewhat different), etc.

Plates LXXXVII and LXXXVIII (sheets 105, 106) Morisco travelling with wife and child in the kingdom of Granada

"In this manner the Morisco goes with wife and child across country or in his garden in the city of Granada, for they have many beautiful gardens with all kinds of unusual fruit."

"In this manner the woman travels with her husband and child across the country."

The man in gray cap with green facing; half blue, half red, silver embossed coat; white girdle with black, gold embroidered pocket; the brown legs naked; feet in brownish sandals or shoes with thongs. The woman in violet, silver embossed mantle; red, silver embossed undergarment and blue stockings; the child in yellow jacket, holds in its left hand, which alone is visible, three white onions with green tops. The basket is yellowish-brown, the mule white with gray hoofs and red breastband, black bellyband and bridle, the latter ornamented with a green tassel on a golden button; saddle grayish-black and edged with gold.

Cf. Heldt, sheet 358b and 359a: Text in the main the same, but Heldt's representation makes a more original impression; the man's face is much more expressive, the yellow branch of the tree more detailed, the landscape beautifully presented with stones and bushes, but the man's right arm is badly drawn. Cf. also Braun and Hogenberg I, 5, middle foreground; II, 3, right foreground, etc., as to the woman riding the ass with her child, which is completely naked in Heldt's picture.

Plates LXXXIX and XC (sheets 107, 108) The Morisco dance

"In this manner the Moriscos dance with each other, snapping with fingers at the same time."

"This is the Morisco dance music they make noises also like calves." (Text mutilated.)

The drummer in green cap with red facing; green, silver embossed coat, blue girdle with red, gold embossed pocket ornamented with two golden buttons; the rock (or sack?) upon which he is sitting is white, gray in the shade, silver embossed; the drumsticks are yellow, gold embossed, the drumhead yellowish, the rest of the drum grayish white with yellow checks. Fiddler with dark violet cap, red, gold embossed coat; fiddle and bow yellowish brown. The third musician in blue, silver embossed coat, which has gold embossed sleeves with yellowish, gold embossed facings; his instrument steel-gray. The dancer in red cap, with violet facing, violet, silver embossed mantle, yellowish, gold embossed coat. The female dancer with white head cloth, red, gold embossed band across her forehead, blue overgarment, white and red undergarment, gold embossed on both sides and with corresponding sleeves, the right sleeve white with red facing, the left red with white facing; violet short stockings. The shoes of all four men yellowish brown.

Cf. Heldt, sheet 360a: "This is the Morisco dance." Heldt's representation is joined on a single sheet, or perhaps it would be better to say that Weiditz has given more room to the figures, but in the main the two are alike, except that in Heldt's picture the man at the right with yellow staff and gray ring is not smooth-faced but has a black moustache and full beard, and also a much different attitude and position, which is probably nearer to the original. The position of the violinist is also different, not facing toward the left; Heldt shows the drummer looking smilingly straight ahead, and his drumsticks have a slenderer form. Weiditz and Heldt are nearest together in the dancing couple.

The Morisco dance, which became fashionable in the first half of the 16th century also in the rest of Europe, including Germany, is referred to with extraordinary frequency in literature. Of the manuscripts preceding Christoph Weiditz's costume-book I draw attention here only to the diary of Dr. Johannes Lange (page 422). So far as I know, a plain, clear representation has heretofore never been published. Reference can also be made in passing to the Morisco dancers of Erasmus Grasser in the Rathaus (city hall) at Munich and the Morisco dances (Morris dance) in England, as to which see M. Dametz, Englische Volkslieder und Moriskentänze, Vienna, 1912, and Ludwig Pfandl, Spanische Kultur und Sitte des 16. und 17. Jahrhunderts, Kempten 1924, page 183. The subject is worthy of a more thorough investigation and depiction.

Plate XCI (sheet 104) Morisco carrying bread

"Morisco man called in their language machaa—" (the rest of the inscription has been cut off).

Chief figure in blue coat and brown girdle, golden buckle, steel-coloured tongue and red pocket, ornamented with two golden buttons; brown sandals over yellowish-brown, high-heeled shoes; the other figure in red, silver embossed dress. Door-opening and four of the loaves of bread brownish, the other two white, the boards yellowish, the house wall brownish.

Cf. Heldt, sheet 359b: "When the Morisco women set their unbaked loaves of bread before the housedoor, they let them remain there until a man goes by, it is his duty according to their law to carry them to the oven, and when they are baked he must bring them back again to the house."

Heldt is doubtless much closer to the original both in his more extended text and in the picture. The attitude of the man is somewhat different, (more natural by Weiditz) and in Heldt's picture there are three loaves on the board which the woman is holding. The window opening through which she reaches out this board is about half the height of a man from the earth in Heldt's picture, which was undoubtedly closer to the reality. Weiditz shows everywhere a tendency to make his pictures more artistic and anatomically more correct, whereas Heldt mainly follows more slavishly the same original, which obviously emphasised more strongly the purely material.

Plate XCII (sheet 60) Dress worn by women in Seville

"In this manner the women go about the kingdom of Marcilia (?) in Seville, the city with 50 thousand houses."

The bonnet black with golden rings and ties; the ornament is a grayish stone, set in gold and surrounded by white pearls; ornamentation on neck and breast, edge of the dress, girdle, bow, half-moon shaped trimming of dress and shoes white and gold embossed; the shoulder cloth white and brown striped, the uppergarment crimson, with large pomegranate shaped decoration in silver and a broad, silver trimming at the height of the knee; sleeves blue with white, silver embossed puffs and ruches; undergarment grayish-violet; the fan alternately from the middle outward red, white, green, white, with golden handle.

No counterpart. I have not been able to learn what is meant by the kingdom of Marcilia.

Plates XCIII and XCIV (sheets 24, 25) Riders in Valladolid

"In this manner they take their wives out riding in Vollodoliff behind them."
Supplementary inscription: "Esclauer" (slave).

The man with black cap, green undergarment underlaid with reddish-violet at the armholes; green breeches and blue mantle; the woman in black hat and mantle with crimson, gold embossed sleeves; the slave in black blouse, with crimson, silver embossed sleeves and crimson breeches; the grayish-white mule with gray hoofs; black, gold decorated bridle, steel-coloured stirrup; point of the spur also steel-coloured.

No counterpart.

Plate XCV (sheet 18) Woman in Galicia (? or Dalmatia) going to the spinning room

"In this manner the women in Galicia go to the spinning house and across the country."

Head dress with the three spindles yellowish, head cloth white, silver embossed; neck chain with one red and two grayish-blue beads alternating; pendant with a red centrepiece on a golden disk, surrounded by grayish-blue pearls; shoulder cloth dark brown, dress blue, silver embossed, with white facings gold embossed on the sleeves and silver embossed on the breast; red, gold embossed girdle, white, silver embossed apron; shoes red, gold embossed; distaff with green socket, surrounded by white fringes, on a yellowish shaft.

Cf. Heldt, sheet 259a: "A common woman in Dalmatia," which is in important details an exact counterpart, though the neck ornamentation is worn on the naked neck, and the headband and also the sandals (each with two thin laces) have obviously not been correctly understood by Heldt. Weiditz is thus doubtless nearer the original in text and picture. But to what region can we assign the spinstress with her three spindles on her head? In the later costume-books the figure appears for instance with Bertelli (Venice 1563), sheet 32, as "Dalmatica vxor," while Vecellio (1589), sheet 271b—text on sheet 272a—designates a quite different woman, who, however, wears the same high sandal-shoes, as "Matrona di Galicia": "Le matrone nobili di Galitia usano quest' habito già ancora dalle Baronesse a principali donne di Spagna, se bene sono differenti nel cappello, il quale è molto largo . . .e i Zoccoli sono all' usanza Spagnuola, come si vede nel ritratto." I regard it nevertheless as probable that our spinstress was originally from the Spanish-Galicia and that the confusion arose later in the costume-books.

Plate XCVI (sheet 123) Woman going to church in Santander

"In this manner the women in Santander go to church."

Mantle and hood bright crimson, silver embossed; uppergarment reddish-gray, silver embossed; undergarment and sleeves red, gold embossed; rosary yellowish-gray, gold embossed. Cf. Heldt, sheet 293a, which is a precise counterpart.

Plate XCVII (sheet 117) Dress worn by old women in Santander

"In this manner the old women dress in Santander in Biscay."

Hat and head cloth white, silver embossed; girdle yellowish, gold embossed. No counterpart.

Plate XCVIII (sheet 124) Dress worn by women in the mountains of Santander and among the Basques

"In this manner they go also in the mountains in Santander also in Biscay."

The whole head decoration and breast cloth white, silver embossed; jacket blue, silver embossed, with red facing and red, gold embossed bodice; girdle golden with silver edging; dress reddish-violet, silver embossed; apron yellowish with red, gold embossed rectangles; shoes yellowish with crimson, gold embossed leather bindings. Cf. Heldt, sheet 292b, which is in the main the same, except that in his picture the woman's left hand does not rest on her back.

Plate XCIX (sheet 95) Woman's dress in Pamplona (Navarre)

"In this manner the women go about in Pamplona or the kingdom of Navarre."

Head dress white (gray in the shade), silver embossed; breast covering brown, uppergarment blue, silver embossed, with gold facing at the sleeve and golden edging; golden girdle; undergarment red, striped with black. Cf. Heldt, sheet 288b: "In this manner the women go about in Pamphilia," which is in the main the same, except that the bonnet merges directly into the white breast cloth. Weiditz's text is nearer the original.

Plate C (sheet 110) Woman's dress in Pamplona (Navarre)

"In this manner the women also go about in the kingdom of Navarre or Pamplona."

Head dress and neck ruffle white, silver embossed; bodice blue, sleeves and dress green, silver embossed; apron white, silver embossed with red edging. Cf. Heldt, sheet 292a, which is again the same, except that the woman has her left hand under the apron, which is white, but with fire-red edging. Heldt's neck ruffle is also improbably thick, almost like a millstone collar. Weiditz is probably nearer the original.

Plate CI (sheet 111) Woman's dress in Pamplona (Navarre)

"In this manner they also go about in the mountains in Navarre."

Head dress and breast cloth white, silver embossed; mantle red, silver embossed, white at the bottom, gold embossed; sleeves green, silver embossed; dress blue, silver embossed; shoes yellowish, gold embossed, with red leather bindings; the socket of the white distaff steel-coloured, the handle light brown.

Cf. Heldt, sheet 289b, which is almost exactly the same, except that the high sandals are completely black, and the distaff, without apparent motive, ends in a large, green heraldic lily reminiscent of a halberd; the white neck cloth is in folds.

Plate CII (sheet 113) Dress worn by Navarre and Basque women in the mountains

"In this manner the women go about in the mountains in the kingdom of Pamplona on the Biscayan frontier."

Head dress and breast cloth white, silver embossed; undergarment blue, silver embossed, with red, gold embossed girdle; sleeves white, silver embossed; dress red, gold embossed.

Cf. Heldt, sheet 284a, which is almost a precise counterpart, except that the drawing leaves much to be desired.

Plate CIII (sheet 131) Costume worn by Basque unmarried women

"In this manner the maidens in Biscay go about before they are wed."

Mantle white, silver embossed; brownish open-work breast cloth; bodice red with double gold stripe as trimming; dress green, silver embossed; the stripes and checks of the white, silver embossed apron red with blue, round spots; hair blond.

Cf. Heldt, sheet 285a, which is an exact counterpart, except that the neck is free, which may have been the original. These "shorn" Basque maidens, who obviously strongly attracted the attention of travellers, are found from this time in literature. Cf. the pictures of Braun and Hogenberg II, 8 ("Bilvao"), where the two girls on the left side of the group of figures are otherwise different; Weigel (1577), page CLV, which also comes into consideration for the following Weiditz sheet; the references in the travel description of Sebald Örtel of 1521/22 (reports of the Germanic National Museum 1896, page 70, concerning "Wayana," that is, Bayonne: "and the maidens are all shorn"), and of Dr. Johannes Lange of 1526 (page 411 et seq.): "In these mountains lies the land of the Basques, which has an impolite people and a peculiar language, which has nothing in common with the languages Italian, Latin, French, German and Spanish, and where the maidens are all completely shorn." A similar remark is found on page 429 during the return voyage in Victoria: "This land has beautiful women and closely shorn maidens and a peculiar language, which is not mixed with and cannot be compared with that of any other country."

Plate CIV (sheet 132) Costume worn by unmarried Basque men

"In this manner the young unmarried men go about in Biscay."

Cap and blouse green, silver embossed; cape grayish violet with reddish stripes, silver embossed; breeches white, silver embossed, with broad, red, gold embossed beadings; sword grayish black with silver trimmings on a blue girdle.

Cf. Heldt, sheet 285b, which shows strong differences. The young man has thrust his right hand into the opening of his blouse at his breast, the black sword with false hilt hangs on a strap which comes forward quite unexplainably from under the left arm, and the costume is not in complete agreement. Cf. also Weigel (1577), page CLV, and as last development, "the expressionist" drawing in the periodical "Wieland," V (1919/20), Nr. 10, page 7.

Plate CV (sheet 133) Basque peasant with his accoutrement

"In this manner the peasants go about with their arms in Biscay."

Hood and blouse yellowish-brown, silver embossed; sleeves and breeches reddish, silver embossed; arrows yellowish with steel-coloured heads, the crossbow grayish-white, silver embossed, with steel-coloured bow and gaffle; the sword black.

Cf. Heldt, sheet 352a, which is nearly the same. However, the peasant here has three arrows in his left hand, a rope attached to his girdle can be plainly seen, and he wears, strange to say, only sock-like shoes, white with yellow cross stripes which are notched above and hence doubtless represent leather. Thus Heldt probably is nearer the original, at least more detailed. His peasant with his arms appears in much the same form in many of the later costume-books—Weigel (1577), page CLVI; Kretschmar and Rohrbach, Die Trachten der Völker, II ed., 1882, plate 71, 8 (text on page 290), and down to the artist of the periodical "Wieland" V (1919/20), Nr. 10, page 19.

Plate CVI (sheet 134) Basque warrior

"In this manner the soldiers look in Biscay."

Cap, codpiece and breeches red, silver embossed; jacket green, lower part of sleeves blue; shield white, silver embossed; with red, silver embossed edge and cross; sword black with steel-coloured, silver embossed cross-guard and reddish, gold striped hilt; lances with steel-coloured heads and yellowish-brown shafts.

Cf. Heldt, sheet 307b, which is similar in attitude and equipment, but varies greatly in details and is without doubt more detailed in the drawing. Thus the lance at the front ends plainly in a four-cornered head; the one at the back, which is not completely visible in Weiditz's picture because the sheet has been cut, ends in a point or blade with a sort of barb and has a red puff below it. Heldt's warrior is also walking more strongly than Weiditz's.

Plate CVII (sheet 121) Dress of fashionable Basque women

"In this manner the rich women dress in Biscay."

Head dress, breast cloth and apron white, silver embossed; uppergarment dark crimson, gold embossed, blue at the bottom, with blue girdle; undergarment blue.

Cf. Heldt, sheet 293b, which corresponds only in some degree to Weiditz's CVII and CXIV, but is somewhat nearer the latter, except that in Heldt's picture a frontal pose with the head turned to the right predominates. Weigel (1577), page CLVIII, is similar. The Biscayan women with their characteristic head dress, quite differently dressed otherwise than Weiditz shows them, play a respectable rôle also in the other costume pictures of the 16th century. Cf. Braun and Hogenberg II, 8; II, 9; V, 16; Bartolomeo Grassi, Dei veri ritratti degl' habiti di tutte le parti del mondo, etc. (Rome 1585), plate 26 (the second of the four women's pictures: "Bilbao"); Vecellio (1589), sheet 261b (text on sheet 262a), 263b, etc.

Plate CVIII (sheet 114) Dress worn by Basque women

"This is also a costume of the women in Biscay."

Head dress and breast cloth white, silver embossed; wrap beneath grayish-yellow, silver embossed; uppergarment violet, silver embossed, with golden edging on the upper sleeves; middle of sleeves and cuffs white, silver embossed; lower part of sleeves violet, silver embossed; girdle gray, undergarment white with blue edging.

Cf. Heldt, sheets 281b and 289a, which, however, are only in general respects the same. Heldt's 289a is nearer to our sheet, but the figure is still more bent.

Plate CIX (sheet 126) Basque women going to church

"In this manner the women in Biscay go to church with reverence, for they are very pious people."

Head dress white, silver embossed, above a yellowish knot; breast cloth white, silver embossed; uppergarment reddish-violet, silver embossed; undergarment red, gold embossed; rosary yellowish, silver embossed.

Cf. Heldt, sheet 282a: "This is also a pious woman who goes to church in Biscay with reverence." The agreement is fairly exact, except that Heldt shows the figure altogether in frontal position.

Plate CX (sheet 118) Old Basque woman going to church

"In this manner some of the old women go to church in Biscay."

Head dress gray with red, gold embossed tassel and silver facing; neck cloth white, silver embossed; mantle crimson, silver embossed; dress red, gold embossed.

Cf. Heldt, sheet 279b, which is almost the same.

Plate CXI (sheet 120) Holiday dress of Basque women

"In this manner the women in Biscay go about on holidays in the house and on the streets."

Head dress, neck cloth and breast covering yellowish-white, silver embossed; sleeves light green, silver embossed, with white, gold embossed facing; bodice blue with golden border, uppergarment red, trimming golden with red, gold embossed and white-bordered circles; undergarment crimson, silver embossed.

Cf. Heldt, sheet 280b, which is nearly the same, except that the peaked bonnet ends in a sort of small cloth crown and the lower edge of the apron has a rosette embroidery, white on a blue band.

Plate CXII (sheet 119) Basque woman spinning

"In this manner they spin in Biscay on the streets and in the house."

Head dress and breast covering yellowish-white, silver embossed; jacket bluish, silver embossed, with red, gold embossed lining and facings; girdle red, gold embossed; uppergarment crimson, silver embossed; undergarment red, gold embossed; distaff and spindle yellowish, the former with red, gold embossed ribbons and brown handle.

Cf. Heldt, sheet 280a, which is nearly the same, except that the head dress is less clearly pictured and the distaff is not stuck under the girdle, but protrudes for no reason at all from behind the back.

Plate CXIII (sheet 116) Basque dancing in Biscaya

"In this manner they dance in Biscay."

Head decoration and breast covering yellowish-white, silver embossed; jacket red, gold embossed; girdle bluish with yellowish-white edgings; lapels of the uppergarment green, undergarment (skirt) violet, silver embossed.

Cf. Heldt, sheet 278b, which is precisely the same. However, Weiditz's figure is much more animated and finer in details, and reproduces much better the attitude of dancing.

Plate CXIV (sheet 125) Basque women's dress in Santa Maria

"Thus they go about in Santa Maria in Biscay."

Head dress yellowish, breast covering white, both silver embossed; jacket light green, silver embossed; girdle golden with white striped edgings; skirt blue, silver embossed; apron white, silver embossed, with two broad red, gold embossed stripes between two narrow gray stripes, with light violet, silver embossed edging.

Cf. Heldt, sheet 293b, which is the same in the main. Cf. also Weiditz's sheet CVII.

Plate CXV (sheet 129) Basque woman's fantastic dress

"This is also a Biscayan woman in her fantastic manner."

Head dress grayish-white, silver embossed, with golden rings and red, gold embossed facing; the open-work breast covering brown, the bodice red, gold embossed, with yellow facing; sleeves grayish-white, silver embossed; uppergarment green, silver embossed; undergarment crimson; upper apron white, strongly gold embossed, red toward the bottom; lower apron white with blue rectangles and circles, between red, gold embossed selvedges.

Cf. Heldt, sheet 283b, which, however, has only a remote resemblance. The woman in Heldt's picture has a much lower cut dress and naked arms, both hands are visible and she appears to be rubbing them together; she faces the front. The word "fantastic" appears to refer to the remarkable head decoration, which goes upward in the form of a spiral staircase in Heldt's picture.

Plate CXVI (sheet 128) Old Basque woman's dress

"This is also an old woman in Biscay, who will not drink apple must."

Head dress yellowish-gray, silver embossed; head cloth red, gold embossed; breast covering white, silver embossed; jacket green, silver embossed; uppergarment blue, silver embossed; undergarment crimson, gold embossed; apron reddish-white, with red squares and bluish points. Staff light brown.

Cf. Heldt, sheet 283a: "This is an old woman in Biscay, who will not drink wine much longer." The pictures are exactly the same, except that in Heldt's picture the face of the woman is more plainly that of an old person and one sees both feet.

Plate CXVII (sheet 115) Dress worn by Basque women in the mountains

"In this manner the women go in the mountains in Biscay."

Head dress and neck cloth white, silver embossed; bodice red, gold embossed; shawl green, silver embossed; uppergarment blue, silver embossed; undergarment yellowish, strongly gold embossed; apron white, silver embossed, with red, gold embossed sprigs as pattern and with the same edging.

Cf. Heldt, sheet 278a, which is in the main the same, except that the neck cloth and head cloth are less well presented and the woman wears around her neck a white cloth with gray stripes.

Plate CXVIII (sheet 122) Dress worn by Basque women in the mountains

"In this manner the women go about at Panta Raouy." (?)

Head dress, breast covering and decorations whitish-gray, silver embossed; shoulders blue, sleeves crimson, silver embossed, with gold facing and lapel trimming; uppergarment crimson, silver embossed, undergarment red, gold embossed; the two uppermost quarters of the apron yellowish-gray, the third yellowish, gold embossed, the undermost yellowish-green, and the whole surrounded by broad, red, gold embossed edging.

No counterpart. I have not been able to discover what locality is referred to.

Plate CXIX (sheet 130) Dress worn by Basque women on the Hispano-French frontier

"In this manner they also go about on the frontier in the mountains in Biscay."

Head dress and breast covering white, silver embossed; the whole uppergarment blue, silver embossed; the whole undergarment and also the lower sleeves red, gold embossed.

Cf. Heldt, sheet 284b, which is almost the same, except that the woman plainly holds her right hand on her back (but probably also in Weiditz's picture), her bonnet is notched above the face and has no tassel at the end.

Plate CXX (sheet 112) Dress worn by Basque women on the frontier and in the mountains

"This is the common costume on the frontier and mountain in Biscay."

Head dress and breast covering whitish-gray, silver embossed; uppergarment blue, silver embossed, yellowish toward the bottom, strongly gold embossed; undergarment red, silver embossed.

Cf. Heldt, sheet 288a. While the woman in Weiditz's picture plainly holds the edge of her mantle with her left hand, which alone is visible, Heldt has obviously not understood the common prototype and has made a spherical-triangular affair of this, through which the blue mantle can be seen.

Plate CXXI (sheet 127) Dress worn by Basque women in the mountains of the French frontier

"In this manner the women go about in the mountains in Biscay on the frontier toward France."

Head dress, breast covering and decoration yellowish white, silver embossed; upper sleeve green, silver embossed; lower sleeve, white, strongly gold embossed, with green facings; uppergarment blue, silver embossed; undergarment red, gold embossed; apron red in the middle, gold embossed, then yellow, gold embossed, then white, silver embossed, and red on the outer edge, gold embossed. The object which she has in her left hand has a green, silver embossed tassel and golden balls.

Cf. Heldt, sheet 282b, which is the main the same, except that the breast covering is less well given and the woman holds in her left hand an unmistakable cord with simple tassel.

Plate CXXII (sheet 91) Women's dress in Roussillon

"In this manner the women go about ordinarily in Rossolonien."

Bonnet white with golden stripes, shawl white, silver embossed, with golden buttons; mantle black, uppergarment dark violet, undergarment red, gold embossed; apron white, silver embossed; the high shoes with alternating white and gold zig-zag pattern.
No counterpart.

Plates CXXIII and CXXIV (sheets 49, 50) Bourgeois dress worn in Roussillon

"In this manner they ride with their wives in Rossolonia."

The man with grayish-violet, silver embossed hat and mantle; green sleeves, grayish-black coat, blue breeches (stockings), with steel-coloured spurs and stirrups; the woman with golden bonnet, brown breast covering, bluish, silver embossed and green edged dress, crimson, gold embossed lower sleeves and red, gold embossed mantle; the first of the two boys in black hat and blouse, crimson, gold embossed lower sleeves and breeches; the shoes which he is carrying in the left hand are brown, white inside; the straps which he is holding in the right hand black; the second boy with brown hat, red, silver embossed blouse, reddish-yellow breeches; the plane (?) which he is holding in the left hand yellowish; bridle of grayish-white mule grayish-brown.
No counterpart.

Plate CXXV (sheet 65) A priest in Roussillon

"This is a priest in Rossolna."

Barret and undergarment black, surplice-like uppergarment white, silver embossed; shawl red, gold embossed; stockings crimson, silver embossed.
No counterpart.

Plate CXXVI (sheet 48) Country woman riding to market in Perpignan

"In this manner the peasant woman rides to market to buy bread and other things in parpingan."

Hat black, hood crimson, breast covering white, jacket yellow with violet facings, dress bluish (spoiled), saddle black, with blue edging at back; bellyband black with steel-coloured rings, reins green, staff yellow, mule and the sack light gray, the three loaves of bread dark brown.
No counterpart.

Plate CXXVII (sheet 93) Women's dress in Languedoc

"In this manner they go about in langedeck on the frontier toward Spain."

The cap black above blond hair, shawl white with grayish-brown ornament, jacket and lower sleeves as well as dress blue, silver embossed, the jacket with broad, gold edging; puffs of the sleeves and apron white, silver embossed; shoes gray and white with bluish, gold edged bands and gold soles; distaff with red socket, spindle grayish-white with black ring.
No counterpart.

Plate CXXVIII (sheet 92) Dance in the district of Narbonne

"In this manner they dance in landadeck by Narbonia."

The dancer at the left with grayish-white head cloth, brown shawl, blue, silver embossed jacket with white puffs, green, silver embossed dress; the dancer at the right with gold head ornamentation, brownish-black shawl, white undergarment, gold embossed around the breast and silver embossed at the arms, and red, gold embossed uppergarment (or mantle?); instrument yellowish.

No counterpart. As to the dance cf. Braun and Hogenberg V, 13 ("Granata") right foreground, where a third female figure with tambourine is seen.

Plate CXXIX (sheet 146) Women's dress in Limousin

"In this manner the women go about in the country in limossyn."

Head dress green in the middle, as also the cloth hanging down; round about a broad, gold embossed band, red above and white below; shawl dark brown; vest green with a golden stripe at the neck; the rest of the dress blue, silver embossed, with white silver embossed puffs and yellowish, gold embossed bows; sandals yellow with black straps, distaff and spindle yellowish, latter with black ring.

No counterpart.

Plate CXXX (sheet 135) Women's dress in Brittany

"In this manner the women are usually dressed in the country of Bretania."

Head dress, collar and apron white, silver embossed; bodice green, silver embossed; lower sleeve red, gold embossed; girdle violet, edged with silver; uppergarment blue, silver embossed; lower garment red, gold embossed.

Cf. Heldt, sheet 287b: "Thus is the dress of the Portanish women as they commonly go in their country." Almost an exact counterpart, except that no girdle is seen, but only the green, white edged apron. Weiditz's text is nearer the original.

Plate CXXXI (sheet 145) Dress of rich unmarried women in France and Hennegau

"In this manner the rich maidens go about in France also in Hennegau."

Bonnet brownish gray with white and golden edging, and with golden stripes; breast covering white, gold embossed; uppergarment crimson, silver embossed, and towards bottom, as also the apron, ermine-white and trimmed with black-white tails; lower sleeves white, stockings crimson, girdle golden, shoes yellowish.

No counterpart.

Plate CXXXII (sheet 94) Girl carrying water in Hennegau

"In this manner the maidens carry water in Hennegau."

Head-pad gray, shawl white with brownish black ornaments; uppergarment light green with golden border, white and strongly gold embossed towards bottom; undergarment bright crimson, silver embossed, with bluish edging at the wrists; upper jar yellowish, lower whitish, with reddish gray pattern.

No counterpart.

Plate CXXXIII (sheet 148) Woman sewing in Hennegau

"In this manner the women in Hennegau sit while they sew."

Mantle blue without, silver embossed, inside white, strongly gold embossed; breast covering dark violet, dress red, gold embossed, with gold border; needlework white; small cushion green, silver embossed, with golden buttons and blue tassels, larger cushion completely grayish violet, gold embossed.

No counterpart.   Since a roll of parchment, containing pattern, appears to be fastened to the sewing cushion, and a small border to the parchment, we probably have here a very early representation of lacemaking by hand, if not the earliest.

Plate CXXXIV (sheet 147) Mixing dough in Zeeland

"In this manner they knead dough in Zeeland."

The woman at the left with white, silver embossed bonnet and similar undergarment; red, silver embossed jacket; cuffs of sleeves white, undergarment blue; the woman at the right with white, silver embossed bonnet, green, silver embossed uppergarment, which appears white, strongly gold embossed, at the bottom and at the cuffs; crimson, silver embossed undergarment; the dough whitish gray, table yellowish, wall reddish yellow with steel-gray fastening of the rolling-pin.
No counterpart.

Plate CXXXV (sheet 149) Bride going to church in Holland

"In this manner the brides go to church in the Netherlands."

Crown golden, bonnet thereunder bluish white with golden bands and ornamental buttons; breast covering dark violet, open work; uppergarment blue, silver embossed, with trimmings of gray fur on the sleeve; undergarment red, gold embossed. Blond hair.
No counterpart.

Plate CXXXVI (sheet 150) Flemish woman going to church

"In this manner the Flemish women go to church."

Mantle black, band across forehead white, rest of dress crimson, silver embossed.
Cf. Heldt, sheet 237a: "A rich woman how she goes to church in the Netherlands." The figure is almost the same, except that the woman is preceded by a small page with a campchair under the left arm and a long bag, probably a purse, in the right hand.

Plate CXXXVII (sheet 151) Dutch women's dress

"In this manner the women generally go about in Holland."

Head dress black with golden trimmings, neckchain golden, breast covering dark violet, uppergarment crimson, silver embossed, with bluish gray edgings and toward bottom (as also at the armholes) apparently lined with gray fur; undergarment yellowish with golden quarterings, girdle golden, veil in the hand white, strongly gold embossed.
No counterpart.

Plate CXXXVIII (sheet 152) Women's dress in Zeeland

"In this manner the women go about in some parts of Zeeland."

Bonnet white, silver embossed; veil (?) grayish white, undergarment (sleeves) blue (badly spoiled). Uppergarment (mantle) black.
No counterpart.

Plate CXXXIX (sheet 153) Women's dress in Friesland

"In this manner the women go about in some parts of Friesland."

Bonnet reddish white, silver embossed, with golden border stripes; undergarment (sleeves) red, silver embossed; uppergarment (mantle) black with golden button.
No counterpart.

Plate CXL (sheet 154) Women's dress in Friesland

"In this manner in some parts the Friesian women are dressed."

Head dress and mantilla black, rest of garment violet, stockings (?) rose.
No counterpart. The same costume and almost the same figure also with Braun and Hogenberg V, 28 ("Flissinga"), right foreground, but the mantle in Weiditz's picture is not so long—almost to the feet—and the position of the hands is different. Similar costume pictures also in Braun and Hogenberg's II, 29 ("Noviomagium"), right foreground; II, 30 ("Campen"), right foreground, in the waggon with nine persons; V, 47 ("Rostochium urbs vandalica Anseatica et megapolitana"), left foreground (with pleated mantle), etc. As to head dress cf. also Weigel (1557), sheet XCI.

Plates CXLI and CXLII (sheets 87, 88) Former German dress

"This was the manner of the noble German clothing some years ago."

The man in red barret with white feather, orange-colored (gold embossed) and white (silver embossed) striped jacket with slit upper sleeves; crimson, light and dark striped, silver embossed lower sleeves; crimson, silver embossed breeches; orange and white striped stockings, trimmed with gray fur; the sword is black, the glass green and three-quarters full of red wine, which shines through; the woman with red cap, orange, gold embossed neckband and bodice; red, silver embossed dress with black border; shawl (shirt), puffs and gloves white, silver embossed; laces of bodice and purse grayish green.
Cf. Heldt, sheet 437b: "The honourable young bachelors went thus clothed in the year 1500." The representation recalls Weiditz's CXLI, but only remotely.

Plate CXLIII (sheet 90) Dress worn by women in Vienna

"In this manner the women in Vienna go about in their dress."

Head dress and mantle grayish black, the latter with golden buttons; kerchief and glove white, dress crimson, silver embossed, with golden buttons.
No counterpart. Vecellio (1589), sheet 319b ("Boema plebea"), with text on sheet 320a, is very similar, especially as regards head dress and neckcloth.

Plate CXLIV (sheet 141) Dress worn by the rich citizens of Genoa

"In this manner the rich burghers in Jennoa go about."

Cap and upper garment (mantle) bright crimson, silver embossed; sleeves green and changing into crimson, silver embossed; stockings (legs and feet) black.
No counterpart.

Plate CXLV (sheet 142) Genoese woman going for a walk

"In this manner the women go walking in Jennoa."

Bonnet yellowish, gold embossed; shawl grayish brown, and above, it would seem, a half-length bodice, deep brown with yellow, gold embossed trimmings; dress proper light green and changing to crimson, with yellow, gold embossed trimmings; under sleeves red, silver embossed; cuffs or ruches at the hands white, gold embossed; apron white, silver embossed, with yellowish, gold embossed trimmings and similar bands, golden balls with gray tassels; the box (?) in the left hand yellowish gray, the feathers of the fan greenish gray with golden handle; as much of the legs as can be seen rose (naked?).
Cf. Heldt, sheet 358a, which, however, is much different. Only the pose and the finish are approximately the same. In Heldt's book here the drawings are continued by a different person with still less artistic understanding. The head, with low-cut waist and undressed, tangled hair, is particularly ugly. The brown colouring of the décolleté may have been added later.

Plate CXLVI (sheet 139) Women's dress in Naples and in the rest of Italy

"In this manner the women go about in the kingdom of Naples and in other places in Italy."

Head decoration golden, breast covering and puffs of the sleeves white, silver embossed; upper garment and the slit sleeves crimson, strongly silver embossed; undergarment blue, fan with black feathers on a golden handle. The page in green, silver embossed jacket and white, silver embossed breeches.
No counterpart. Very similar in pose, bonnet and puffed sleeves and fan is Cesare Vecellio (1589), sheet 72b ("di Venetia e altrove"); text on sheet 73a.

Plate CXLVII (sheet 140) Women's dress in Romagna

"In this manner the women go about in Romania."

Head dress grayish blue (striped), breast covering brown open work, dress brownish violet with golden border and shot through horizontally with golden threads; upper sleeves green, silver embossed; under sleeves bluish, silver embossed; shirt edging white; the fan with black, somewhat gold embossed feathers and golden handle.
No counterpart.

Plate CXLVIII (sheet 143) Women's dress in Venice
Plate CXLIX (sheet 144) Men's dress in Venice

"In this manner the women and men go about in Venice."

The woman's hairnet golden, the open-work breast covering grayish violet, merely indicated; the whole dress grayish black, shot through horizontally with gold threads; shirt edging at throat and hand white, silver embossed. The man in grayish black, only the sleeves of the undergarment blue, the girdle white with golden buttons.

No counterpart. The man resembles to some degree the representation of Bertelli (Venice, 1563), sheet 1 ("Italicae uaenetiae"), but he wears here an ornamented collar which, provided that both sheets go back to a common prototype, may explain the remarkably shaded throat on Weiditz's drawing. The woman's coiffure is similar to that of Vecellio (1589), sheet 71b: "Donne e Spose." The text to this, on sheet 72a, in like manner as Vecellio frequently refers to ancient times, is: "Habito antico di Donne e di Spose."

Plate CL (sheet 137) Women's dress in England

"In this manner the women ordinarily go about in England."

Head dress green above a bluish white, silver embossed band; shawl brown, throw white, silver embossed; uppergarment red, silver embossed, with bluish facings on the sleeves; undergarment light brownish violet, shot through with parallel silver threads.

No counterpart.

Plate CLI (sheet 138) Dress worn by unmarried men in England

"In this manner the young bachelors go about in England."

Cap and jacket light brownish violet, silver embossed; breeches red, gold embossed; shoes light brownish violet with black trimmings; purse white, silver embossed, with golden buttons and handle on golden girdle.

No counterpart.

Plate CLII (sheet 136) Women's dress in Ireland

"In this manner the women go about in Ireland."

Head dress grayish white, silver embossed; shawl brown, open work; uppergarment (mantle) light violet, gold embossed, with red, silver embossed facings and the same lining; undergarment yellowish, strongly gold embossed. Shoes red, silver embossed.

No counterpart. Cf. Braun and Hogenberg VI, 3 ("Hibernia" = Ireland). The "Matrona Hiberniae" corresponds nearly to Weiditz's CLII, except for lack of head dress. Costume and position of the feet and hands are about the same, but the sleeves are somewhat different.

Plate CLIII (sheet 14) Dress worn by the Portuguese

"In this manner the men generally go about in Portugal."

Cap and mantle black, the former with red centre and gold-white buckle, red band and bluish stone (?) set in gold; shirt edging white, gold embossed; breeches yellow.

No counterpart in Heldt's work. But Vecellio (1589), sheet 266b, has about the same figure, with the superscription: "Donna di Granata." And the text on sheet 267a reads: "Habito di donna di Granata," "Mulier Bettica." The Portuguese costumes depicted by Vecellio in sheets 268b and 269b are entirely different. But the picture on sheet 267 is without doubt a man's costume, and hence Weiditz is undoubtedly right in ascribing it to Portugal.

Plate CLIV (sheet 15) Dress worn by Portuguese women

"In this manner the women generally go about in the kingdom of Portugal."

Cap black, with white centre and golden ornamentation; large ornaments, red in the middle, golden and bluish, at ear and neck; neckchain red, shawl dark brown, upper garment crimson with gold edging and trimming; girdle, bow, puffs of sleeves and cuffs white, silver embossed; under-garment and shoes yellowish, the latter with crimson leather; the flowers crimson with greenish stalks.

No counterpart.

APPENDIX

The Coat-of-Arms of Ferdinand Cortez (cf. plate IV)

The quartered armorial bearings which Ferdinand Cortez holds on two rose-coloured ribbons in plate IV present a number of heraldic as well as chronological difficulties and riddles, due in some degree to the sketchy character of the drawing. I am indebted to Dr. Ludwig Rothenfelder, the genealogist and authority on heraldry of the Germanic Museum, for the solution of most of the questions involved. In the consideration of these bearings, which I have assigned to the appendix in order not unnecessarily to interrupt the continuity of the main text, I follow in the main Dr. Rothenfelder's explanations, and I desire at the very outset to express my hearty thanks for his cooperation. Particular thanks are due also to the Archivo Heráldico de los Señores de Rújula, Cronistas Reyes de Armas de S. M. in Madrid for various valuable corrections and additions.

We begin with the first quarter of the coat-of-arms (left upper corner), which is also quartered, and mark these quarterings with a—d. The quartering 1a corresponds with the coat-of-arms of the family Rodriguez de las Varillas and hence with that of "the male line (varonia) of the Cortezes of Monroy" (Archivo Heráldico). The ancient Spanish family of the Monroys flourished already in the twelfth century in Estremadura and was descended, according to some writers, from the kings of Castile. (Cf. Siebmacher's Grosses Wappenbuch I, 3 IIIc, page 176.) The Monroy coat-of-arms, which is merely suggested and not heraldically detailed by Christoph Weiditz, really contains four pales gules on a field or and a border azure studded with eight Latin crosses argent. (Cf. Siebmacher, plate 263; Rietstap, Armorial général.) Hence it is to be regarded as the real coat-of-arms of the Cortez family. (Cf. Rietstap, plate CXXXI, where it appears with the Cortez bearings as inescutcheon).

The quartering 1b is so sketchily and incompletely executed that its meaning cannot be established with certainty. If the middle field should contain a pine and two bears rampant, one on each side, then, according to the Archivo Heráldico, it would be the coat-of-arms of the mother of Ferdinand Cortez, a Pizarro, which, however, is shown by Rietstap without border. So it is possible, according to Dr. Rothenfelder, that we have here to do with the bearings of Medellin in Estremadura, the city where Cortez was born. These bearings contained a stone-coloured castle with three towers, surmounted by a mullet azure with 6 points between two pales or on a field argent, the whole surrounded by a border gules set with eight saltires or. Weiditz indicates only this border.

"The third and fourth quarterings of the first quarter (1c and 1d) correspond," as the Archivo Heráldico reports, "to the coat-of-arms of the Altamirano, the family of Ferdinand Cortez's maternal grandmother (abuela materna), and the figures and tinctures in the quartering 1c are ten hurtes on a field argent, the border gules set with eight saltires or in memory of the participation of the Estremadura in the taking of Baeza. The quartering 1d has a mullet or in chief on a field gules and a rampant lion or in base argent."

The second quarter of the bearings, which shows a bend sable on a field argent and a chain or consisting of eight links, which takes the place of the characteristic border so often encountered in Pyrenaean heraldry, is the coat-of-arms of the Zuñiga de Bejar. Cortez's second wife was Doña Juana de Zuñiga, a daughter of Carlos, the second Count of Aguilar, and a niece of the Duke of Bejar.

We come to the third quarter, at the dexter base. This, too, is not completely executed in its heraldic details, but the fact that it is parted per pale permits the fairly definite assumption that it is intended to be the bearings of the Arellano, which, also parted, show on the dexter side one whole and one half fleur-de-lis gules and on the sinister side a whole fleur-de-lis and the other half fleur-de-lis, here gules in argent. The tinctures are variously given in the heraldic works. As to this, see, for example, Jakob Wilhelm Imhof, Genealogiae viginti illustrium in Hispania familiarum, etc. (Leipzig, 1712), page 1, and also the same writer's Historische, Genealogische, Politische Nachrichten Von denen Grands d'Espagnes Oder Grossen in Spanien, etc. (Bremen, 1718), page 270. Rietstap assigns the bearings to the family Arenala, not to the Arellanos. According to the Archivo Heráldico de los Señores de Rújula in Madrid, however, the original letters patent of nobility of Don Jeronimo Cortés y Arellano, Zuñiga y Arellano, born in the '60's of the sixteenth century, which were issued in the year 1590 and are in the possession of the Archivo, show the above mentioned tinctures, and the ascription of the bearings to the Arellano family is beyond question.

Before taking up the connection of the Arellanos to the Cortez coat-of-arms depicted by Weiditz, let us first complete the consideration of the fourth and last quarter of the bearings. This quarter, which is also imperfectly executed, is intended to represent the personal bearings of Ferdinand Cortez, which, according to the kind report of the Archivo Heráldico, were thus described in the grant made to him by Charles V:

"To the coat-of-arms which you bear as that of your family, you may add as your own and acknowledged bearings a shield showing, in the middle at the right and in the upper part a black, double-headed eagle in a white field — the coat-of-arms of Our Empire — and in the other half of the said shield and in its lower part a golden lion in a red field in memory of the fact that you, the said Ferdinand Cortez, through your zeal and courage have brought affairs to the fortunate conclusion mentioned above; in the other half of the said middle shield, at the left hand above (Weiditz depicts it below) there shall be three crowns of gold in a black field, one above the other (reverse with Weiditz) in memory of the three rulers of the great city of Tenustitan and their countries which you conquered, and the first of whom was Montezuma, who, after you had taken him prisoner, was killed by his own people; and then Cuetaozin, his brother, who succeeded him in the rulership and rose against Us and drove you out of that city again; and the other, who succeeded in the rulership, Guatenemucin, who remained in rebellion until you conquered and captured him. And in the lower part (upper part with Weiditz) of the left half of the said shield you may bear the city of Tenustitan[1] in your bearings, with its fortifications on the water, in memory of the fact that you conquered it by the might of ships[2], and could subject it to Our rule; and on the border of the said shield in a yellow field seven leaders and lords of seven lands and cities, who arose against Us and whom you conquered and made captives in the said city of Tenustitan, may fill up the space, arrested and fettered with a chain which is held together with a lock below the said shield." Weiditz shows eight chieftains instead of seven, whom Dr. Rothenfelder is inclined to regard as representing the Indian princes and cities subjugated by Cortez — Tabasco, Mexico, Caziku, Flascalen, Cholula, Tezcuco, Taccuba and Honduras (?). The real bearings, or, as they are called in the imperial privilege, the middle shield, is given more correctly

---

[1] Cortez had sent Emperor Charles V a picture of this city of Tenustitan, Tenochitlan or Temixtitan, the capital of the country, the Mexico City of today, which is situated on two lakes with floating gardens. Fragments of this picture are still preserved in the National Museum of Mexico.

[2] That is to say, Cortez's brigantines, with which he won a victory for Spain against the natives with their more than 500 boats, as he himself reported.

by Rietstap than by Weiditz, cf. Armorial général, plate CXXXI, where the coat-of-arms of the Cortez family figures as the heart-shaped shield referred to.

Thus all the bearings on our coat-of-arms on plate IV can be normally and definitely connected with Ferdinand Cortez except the above described bearings of the Arellanos, which appear in the third quarter (dexter base). These are connected with Cortez only insofar as his own family, and especially the family of his second wife, were related by marriage to the Arellanos. Thus his brother-in-law, Peter IV, Count of Aguilar, married in 1532 the daughter of an elder brother, thus also a brother-in-law of Cortez, who for his part had been married likewise to a Zuñiga, Anna de Arellano, and a daughter of Peter IV and of this Anna, whose name was also Anna, married Cortez's son, Don Martin Cortez Zuñiga, Marquis del Valle, the father of the Don Jeronimo referred to above. (Cf. Imhof, Genealogiae, table II, and written reports of the Archivo Heráldico). It is probable that the connection with the high Arellano family, which was related to the royal house of Navarre, led as early as 1532 to this supplementing of the Cortez bearings, or that the wedding celebration of that year gave occasion to Christoph Weiditz, when he was dealing with the Cortez bearings, to add the Arellano coat-of-arms to them arbitrarily. However, it is also possible that the bearings on our plate IV, the detailed execution of which could point to another hand than the cruder and more energetic hand of Weiditz, were executed considerably later, after the marriage of Martin Córtez with Anna de Arelano. In the last named event, we should see in the Cortez plate a further confirmation of the assumption that Christoph Weiditz devoted himself chiefly in his latter years to woodcuts, for which he may then have also arranged and amplified the sheets of his costume-book.

AUTHENTIC
EVERYDAY DRESS
OF THE
RENAISSANCE

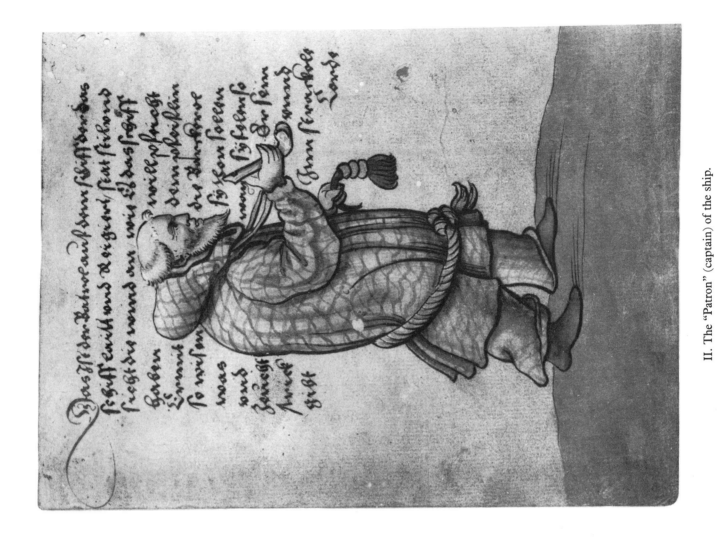

II. The "Patron" (captain) of the ship.

I. Christopher Weiditz in his sailor's dress.

IV. Ferdinand Cortez (Hernán Cortés, 1529).

III. The steersman of the ship.

V & VI. Andreas (Andrea) Doria (1529) and the owner of a Spanish ship.

VII & VIII. Imperial baggage wagon in Castille.

IX. Doña Menzia Zenette of the House of Mendoza.

X. Drummer in the procession of the entry of the Emperor.

XI & XII. Indians playing mora and catch-stone.

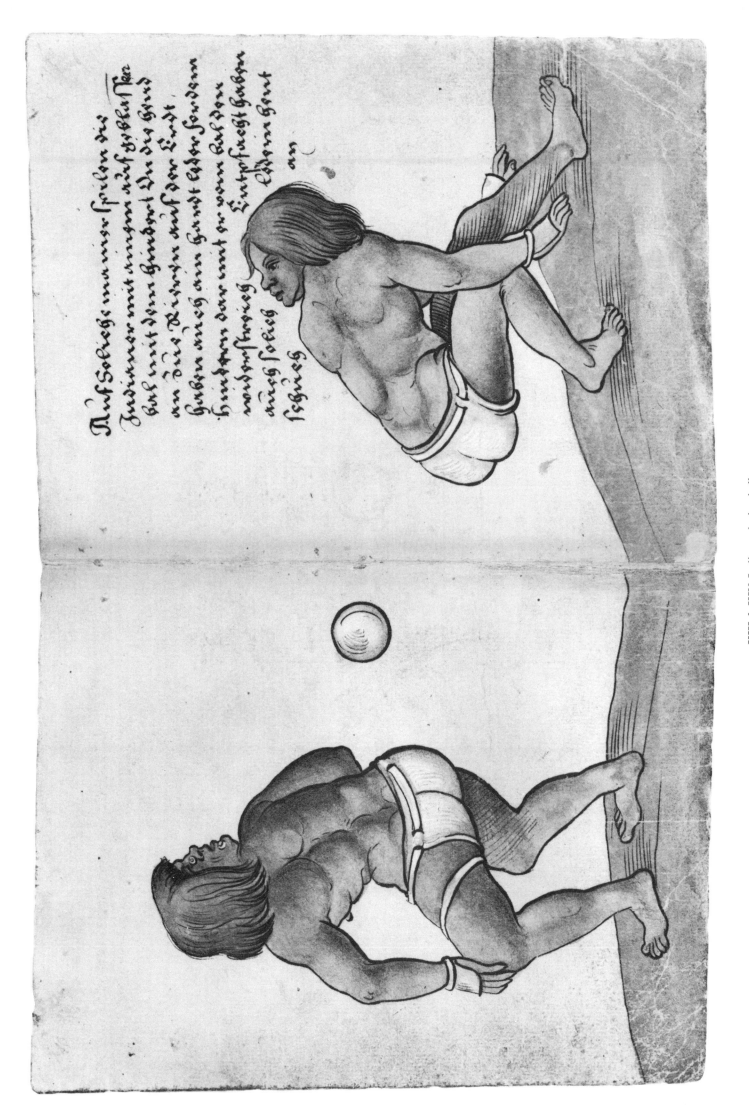

XIII & XIV. Indians playing ball.

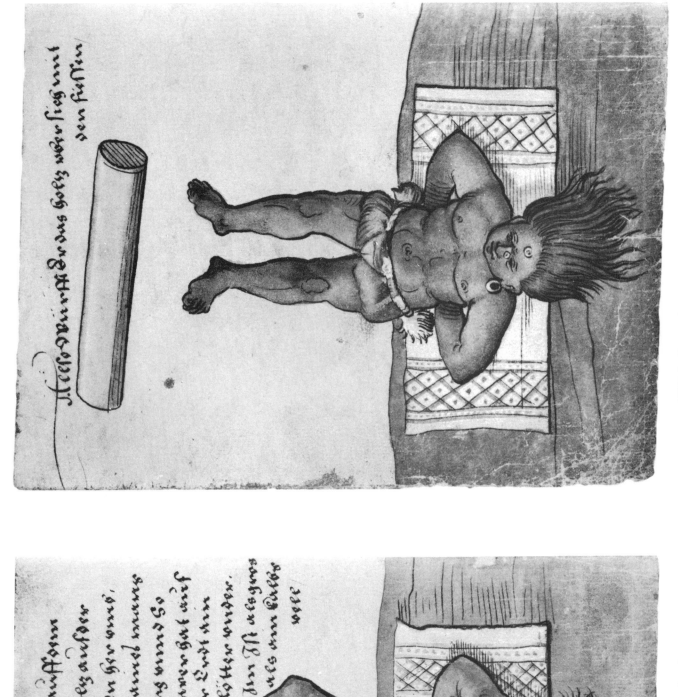

XVI. Indian performance with a wooden block (second phase).

XV. Indian performance with a wooden block (first phase).

XVIII. Indian woman.

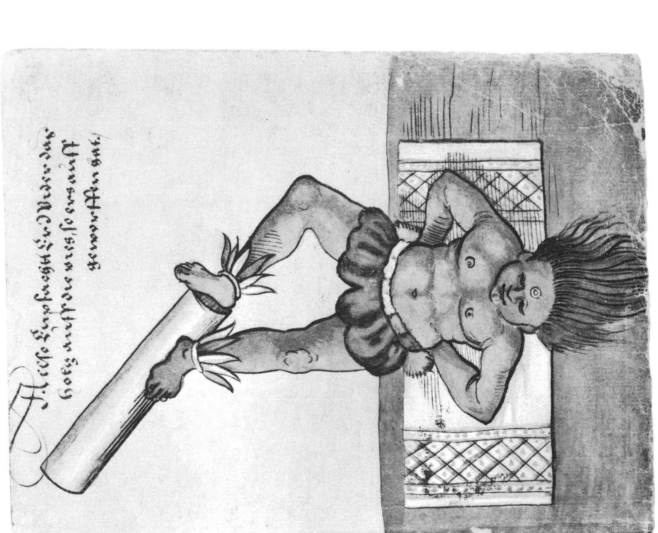

XVII. Indian performance with a wooden block (third phase).

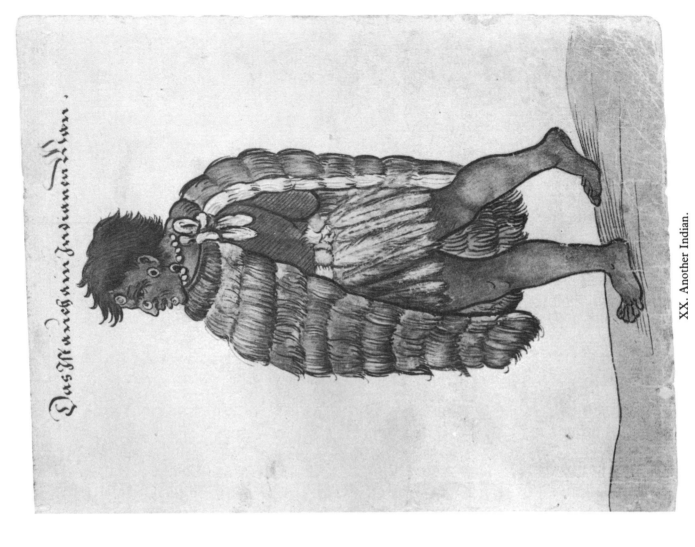

XX. Another Indian.

XIX. Indian man.

XXII. Indian chief ("Noble").

XXI. Indian with a wooden drinking jug.

XXIV. Dress of a rich prelate in Toledo.

XXIII. Indian (?) with his accoutrement.

XXV & XXVI. Transporting wine in Toledo.

XXVII & XXVIII. Toledan prelate riding.

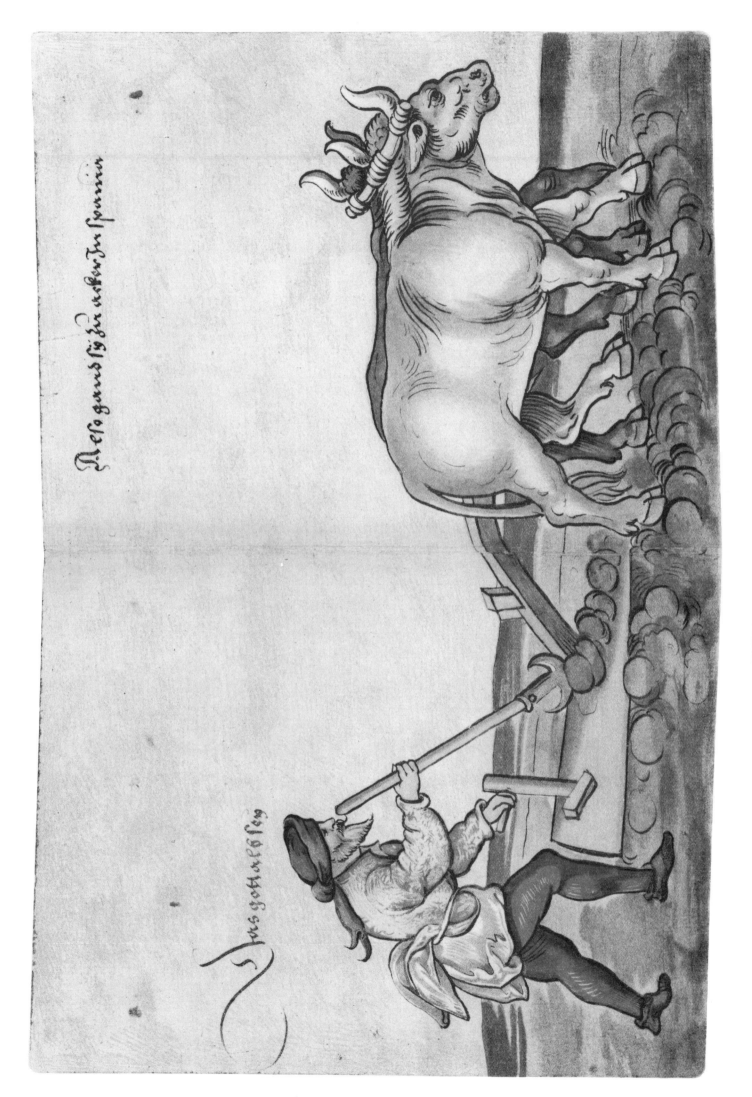

XXIX & XXXX. Spanish peasant ploughing.

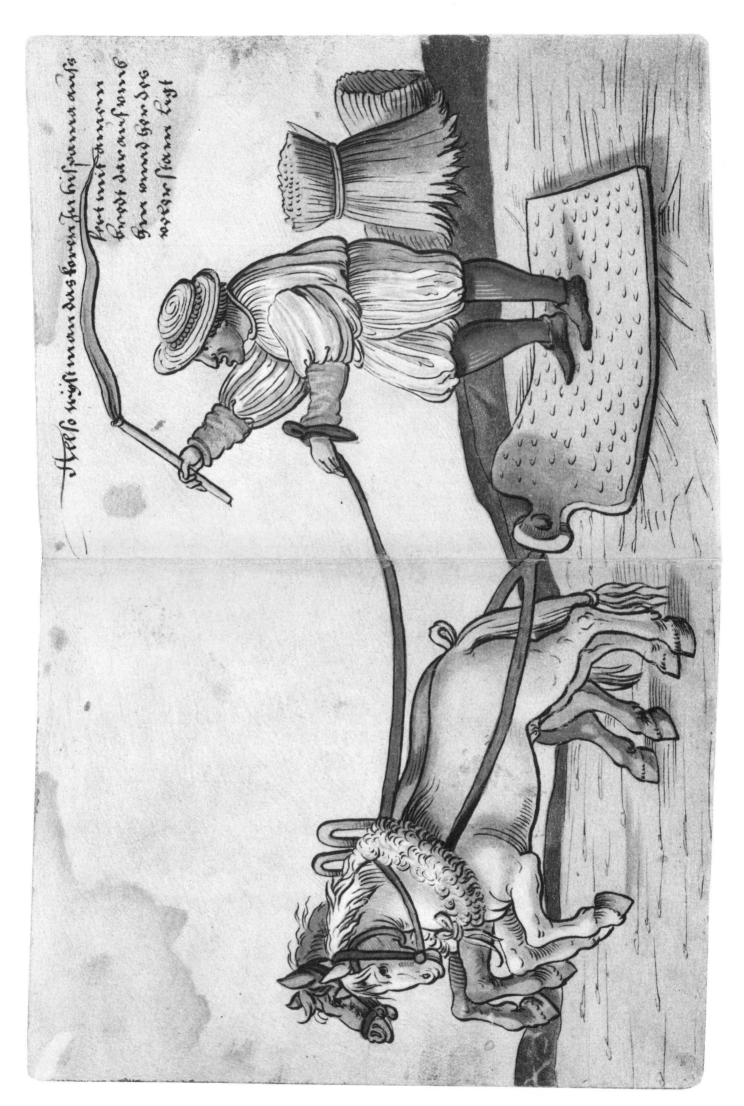

XXXI & XXXII. Threshing corn in Spain.

XXXIV. Transporting corn and flour in Spain.

XXXIII. Cleaning corn in Spain.

XXXV & XXXVI. Castilian water-seller.

XXXVIII. Spanish police officer ("alguacil").

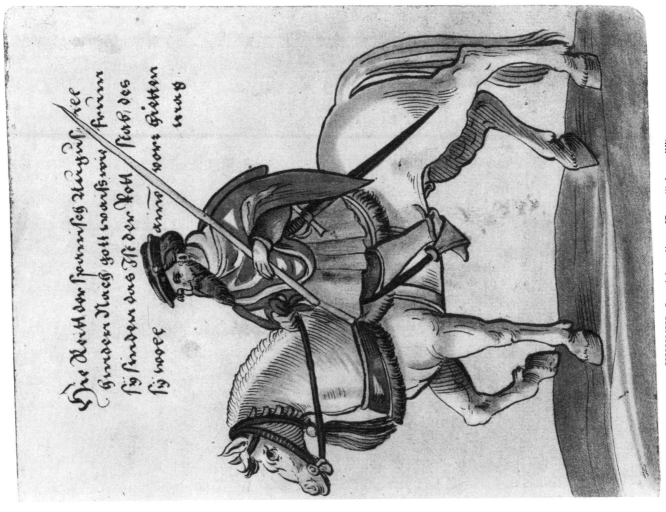

XXXVII. Spanish bailiff.

XXXIX & XL. Spanish court usher; punishing a cut-purse in Spain.

XLII. A Spanish beadle.

XLI. Another Spanish policeman.

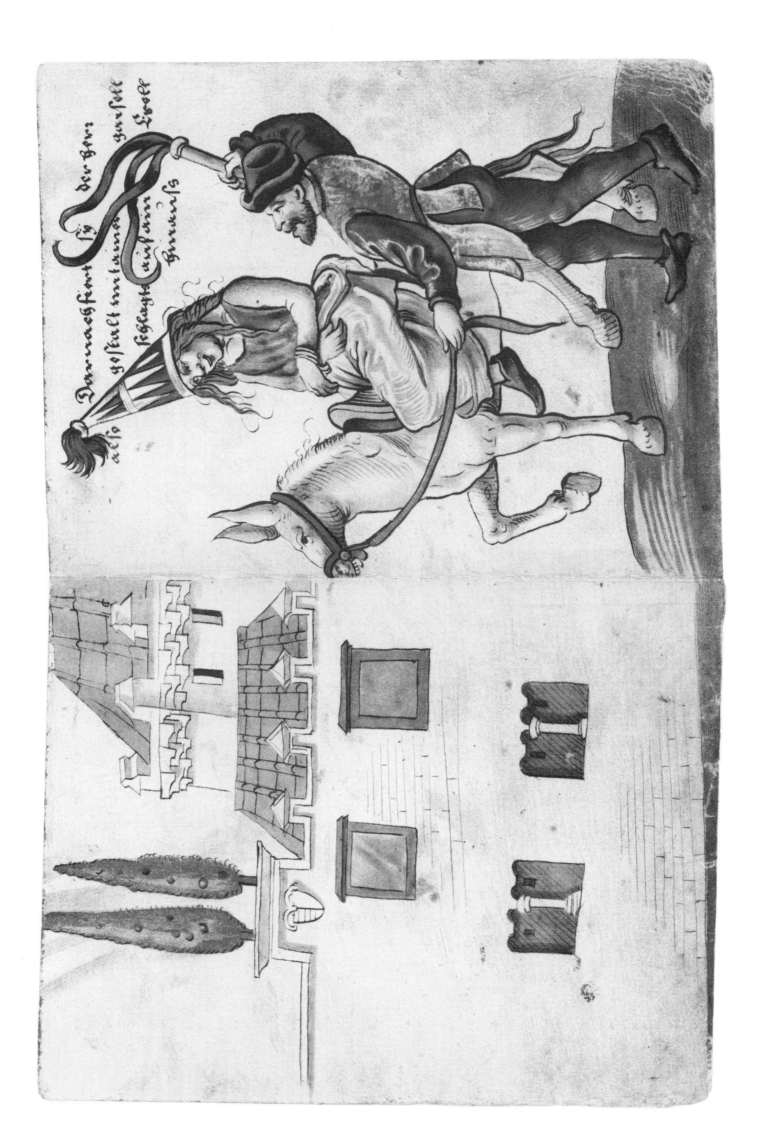

XLIII & XLIV. Flogging a Spanish female criminal.

XLVI. Collector of ransom for the prisoners of pirates.

XLV. Punishing a female criminal in Spain.

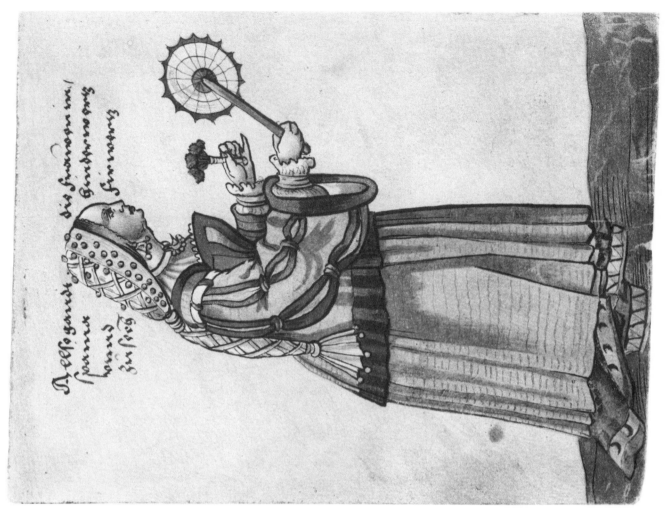

XLVIII. Dress of a Spanish noblewoman.

XLVII. Negro slave with a wine-skin in Castile.

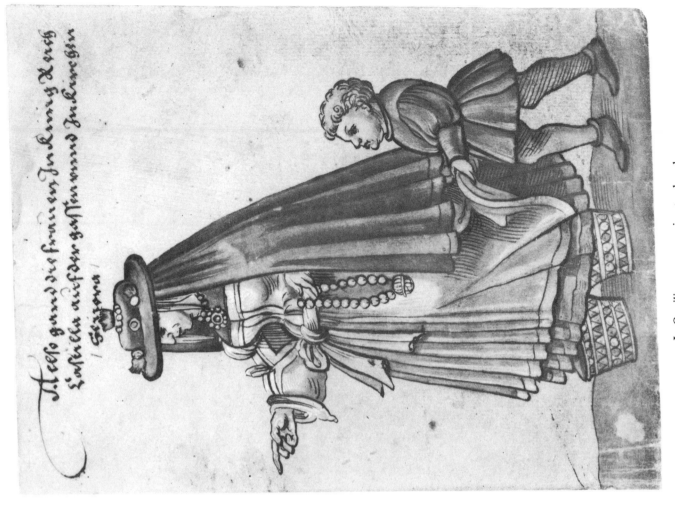

L. Castilian woman going to church.

XLIX. The same dress seen from behind.

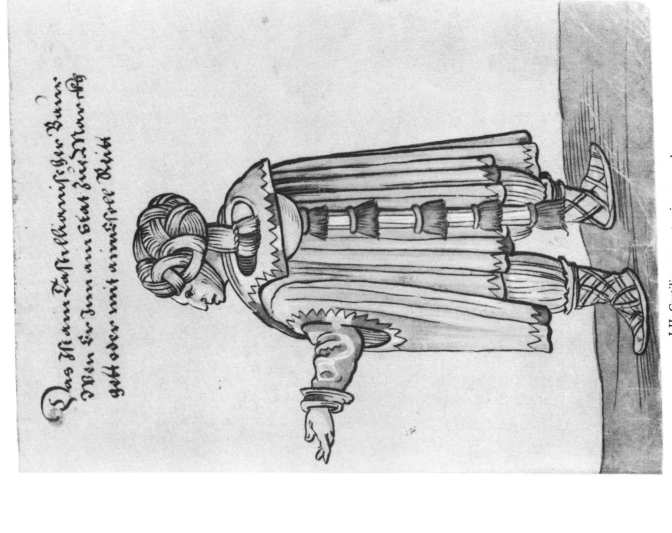

LII. Castilian peasant going to market.

LI. Spanish nobleman riding.

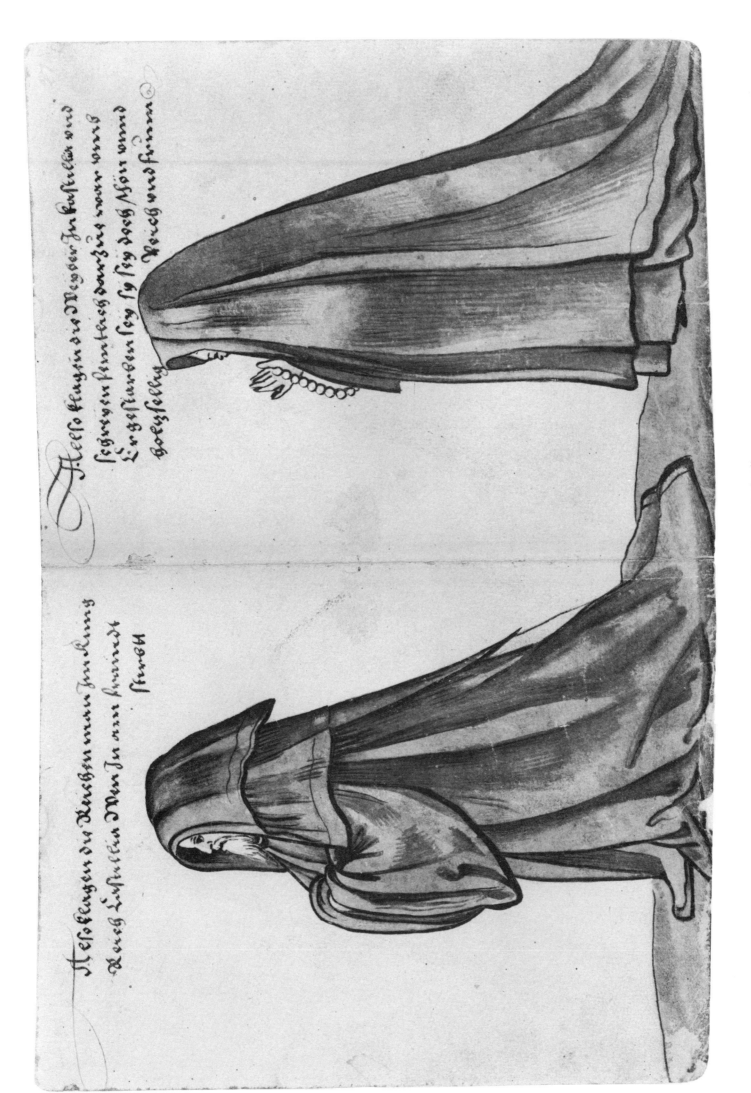

LIII & LIV. Bewailing the dead in Castile.

LVI. Castilian penitent (flagellant).

LV. Castilian shepherd.

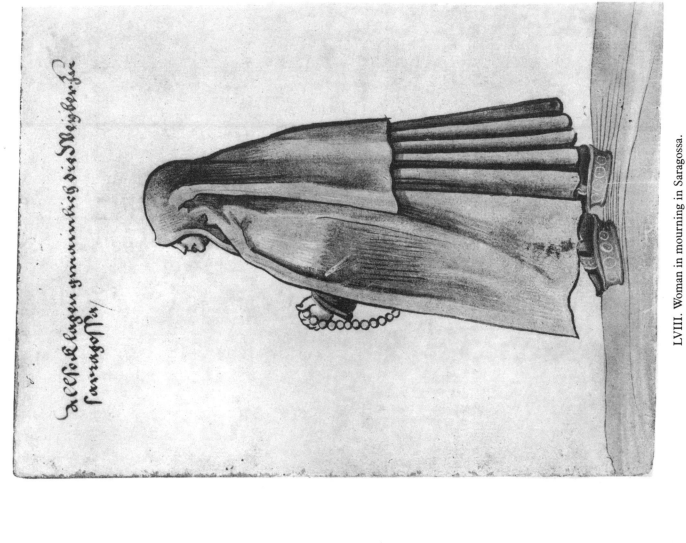

LVIII. Woman in mourning in Saragossa.

LVII. Penitent in Saragossa.

LIX & LX. Tugging boats into the harbour of Barcelona.

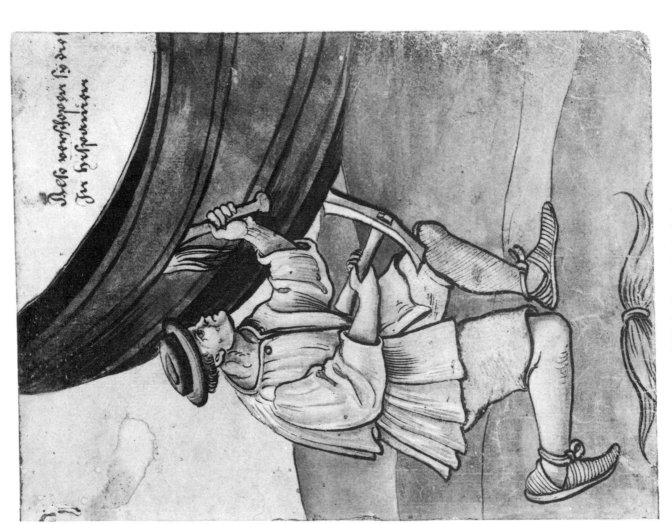

LXII. Loading horses into ships

LXI. Caulking ships in Spain.

LXIII & LXIV. Ships taking in water in Barcelona.

LXV & LXVI. Spanish galley-slaves.

LXVII & LXVIII. Escort of a noblewoman in Barcelona.

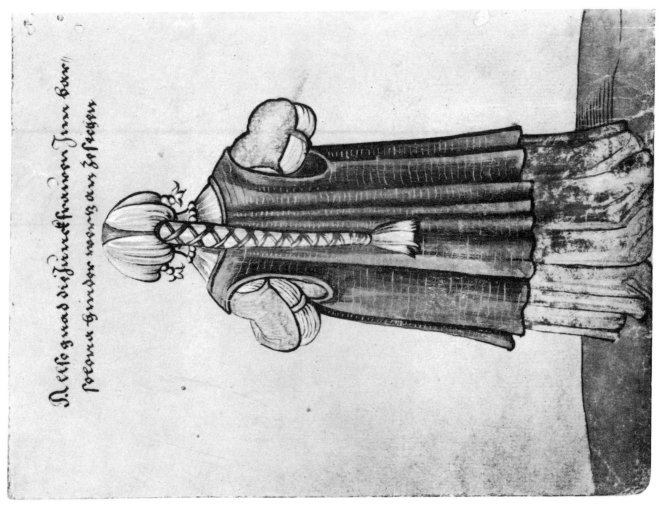

LXX. Unmarried woman in Barcelona, back view.

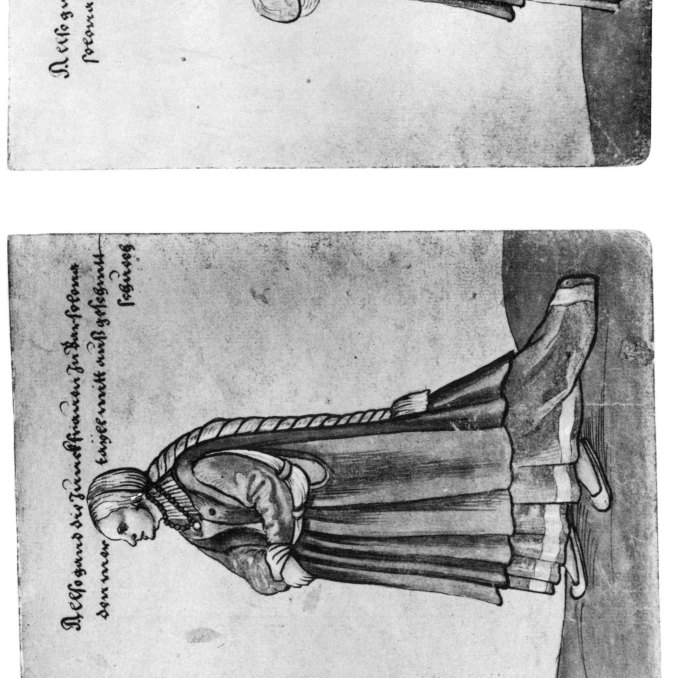

LXIX. Unmarried woman in Barcelona, front view.

LXXII. Woman of fashion going to church in Valencia.

LXXI. Woman's dress in Barcelona.

LXXIII & LXXIV. Catalonian noblewoman in mourning, and Spanish water-carriers.

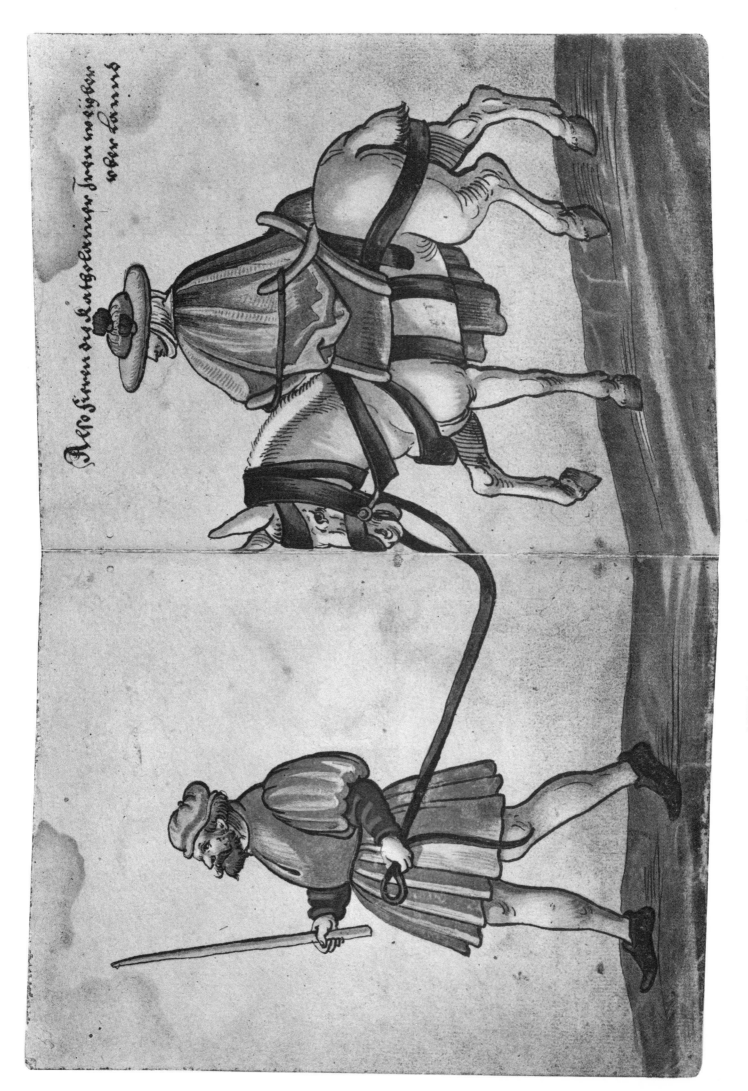

LXXV & LXXVI. Catalonian married couple traversing the country.

LXXVIII. Citizens riding in Valencia.

LXXVII. Woman walking in the kingdom of Valencia.

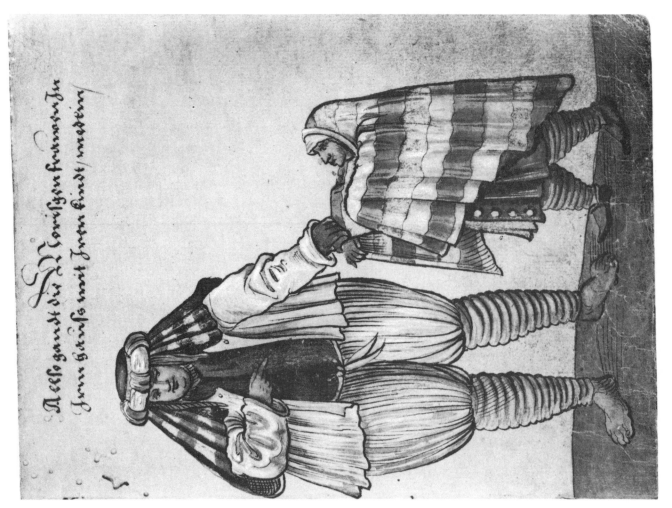

LXXX. House-dress worn by Morisco women and children.

LXXIX. House-dress worn by Morisco women in Granada.

LXXXII. Morisco woman sweeping her house.

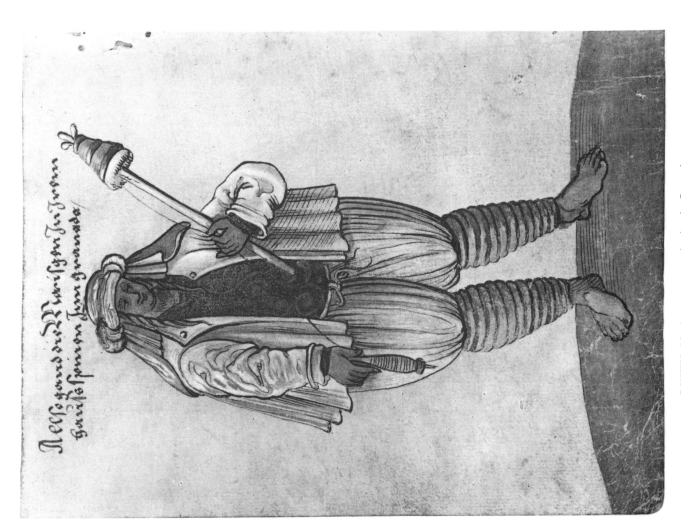

LXXXI. Morisco woman spinning in Granada.

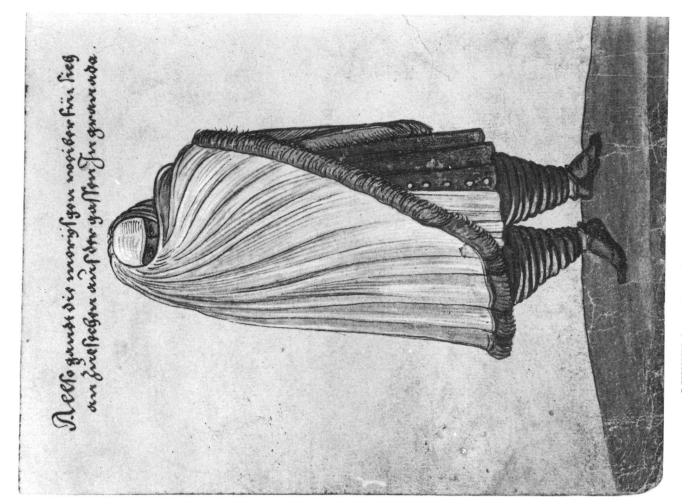

LXXXIV. Street-dress of Morisco women in Granada.

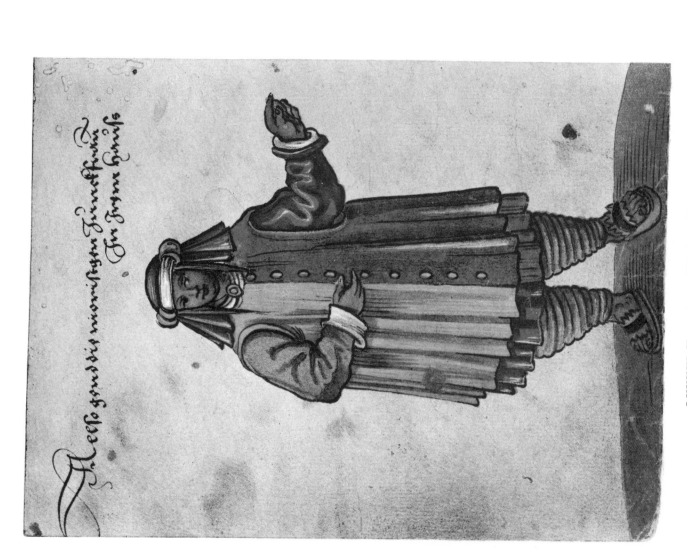

LXXXIII. House-dress of Morisco girls.

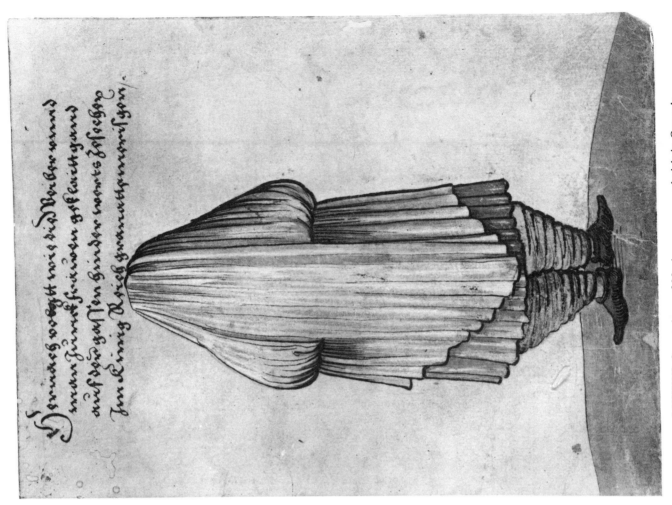

LXXXVI. Street-dress of Morisco women and girls in Granada.

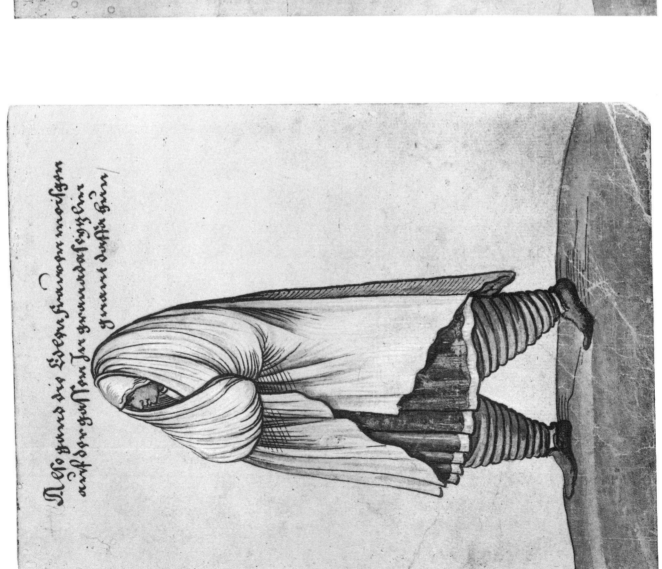

LXXXV. Street-dress of fashionable Morisco women in Granada.

LXXXVII & LXXXVIII. Morisco travelling with wife and child in the kingdom of Granada.

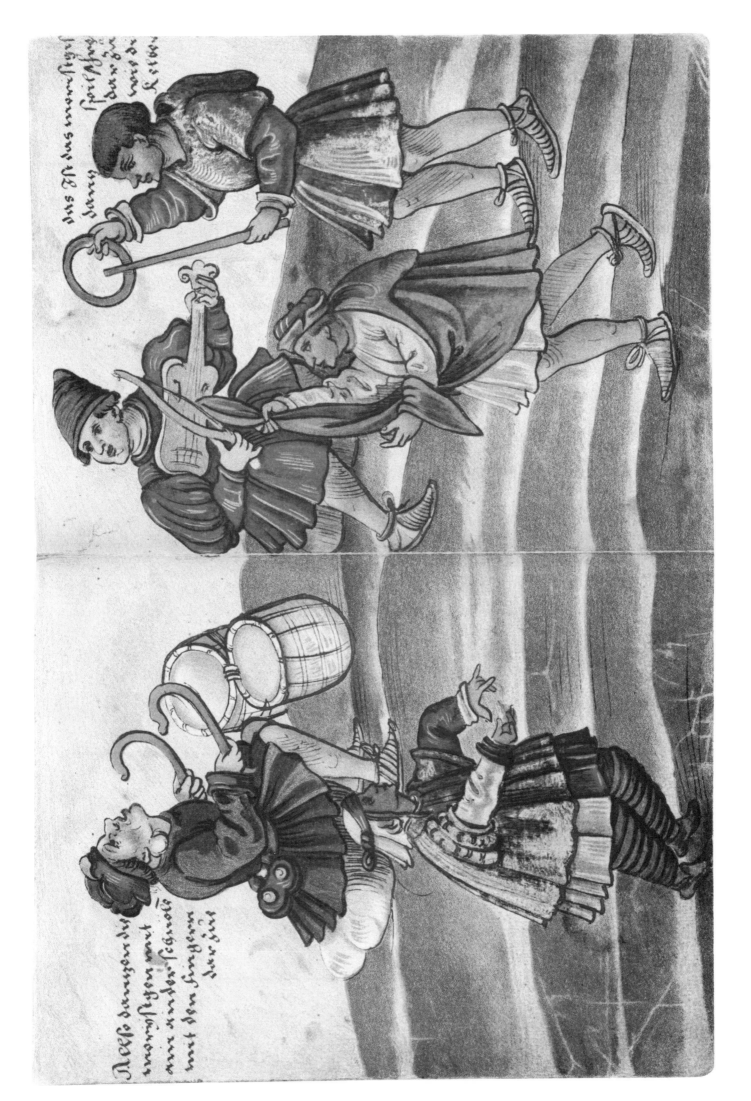

LXXXIX & XC. The Morisco dance.

XCII. Dress worn by women in Seville.

XCI. Morisco carrying bread.

XCIII & XCIV. Riders in Valladolid.

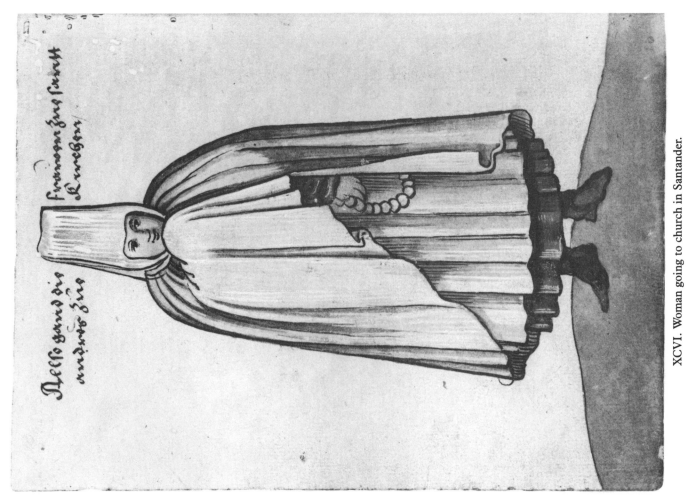

XCVI. Woman going to church in Santander.

XCV. Woman in Galicia (? or Dalmatia) going to the spinning-room.

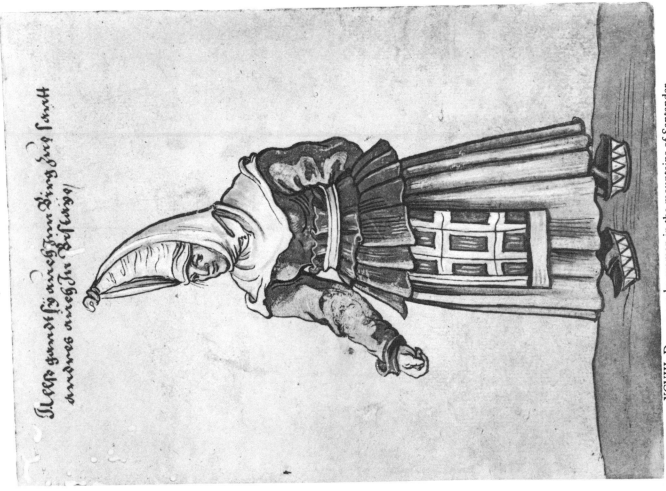

XCVIII. Dress worn by women in the mountains of Santander.

XCVII. Dress worn by old women in Santander.

C. Woman's dress in Pamplona (Navarre).

XCIX. Woman's dress in Pamplona (Navarre).

CI. Woman's dress in Pamplona (Navarre).

CII. Dress worn by Navarre and Basque women in the mountains.

CIV. Costume worn by unmarried Basque men.

CIII. Costume worn by Basque unmarried women.

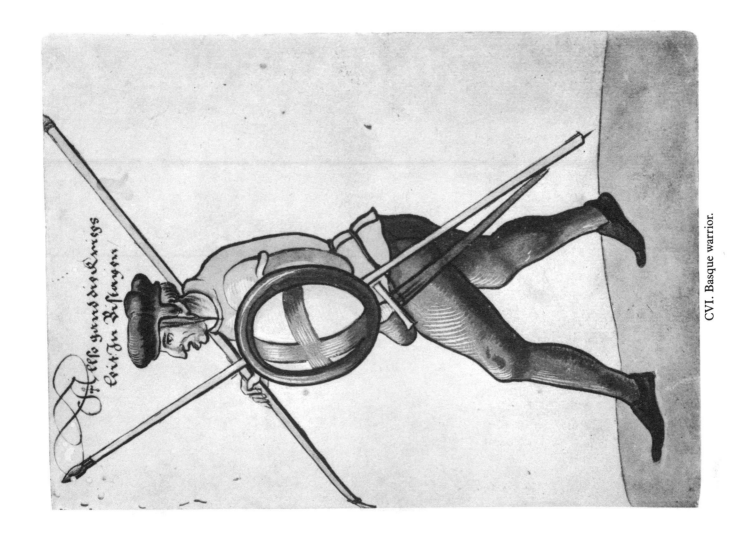

CVI. Basque warrior.

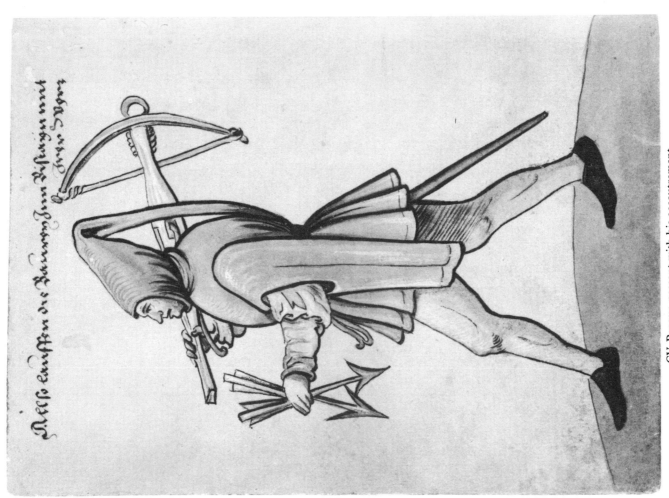

CV. Basque peasant with his accoutrement.

CVIII. Dress worn by Basque woman.

CVII. Dress of fashionable Basque women.

CX. Old Basque woman going to church.

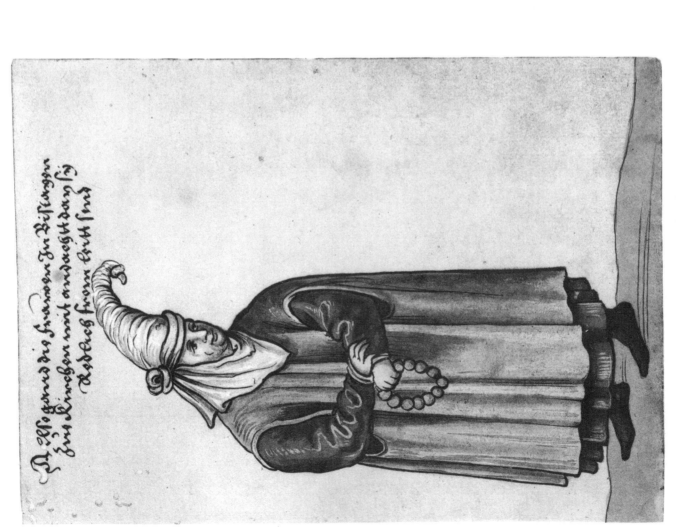

CIX. Basque woman going to church.

CXI. Holiday dress of Basque women.

CXII. Basque woman spinning.

CXIV. Basque women's dress in Sta. Maria.

CXIII. Basque dancing in Biscaya.

CXV. Basque woman's fantastic dress.

CXVI. Old Basque woman's dress.

CXVIII. Dress worn by Basque women in the mountains.

CXVII. Dress worn by Basque women in the mountains.

CXX. Dress worn by Basque women on the frontier and in the mountains.

CXIX. Dress worn by Basque women on the Hispano-French frontier.

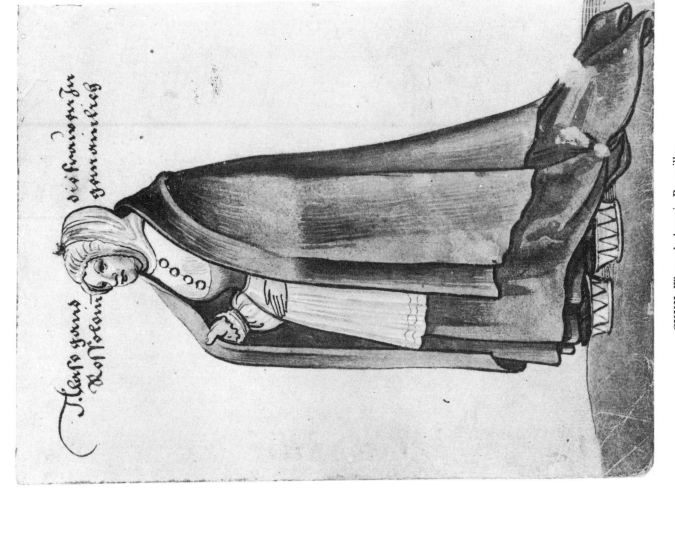

CXXII. Women's dress in Roussillon.

CXXI. Dress worn by Basque women in the mountains of the French frontier.

CXXIII & CXXIV. Bourgeois dress worn in Roussillon.

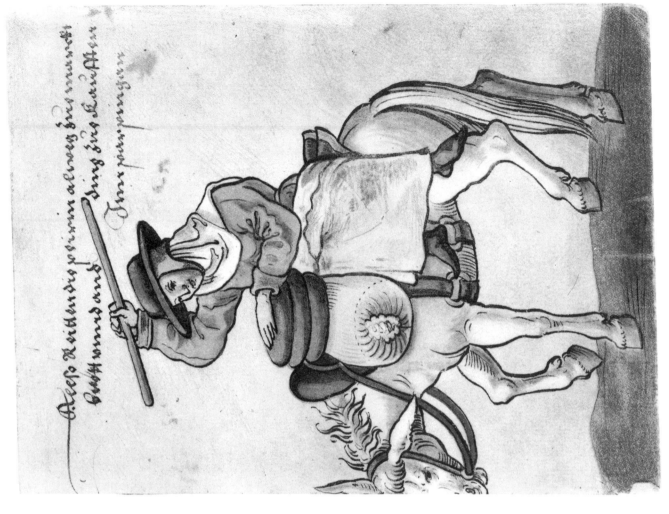

CXXVI. Country-woman riding to market in Perpignan.

CXXV. A priest in Roussillon.

CXXVIII. Dance in the district of Narbonne.

CXXVII. Woman's dress in Languedoc.

CXXX. Women's dress in Brittany.

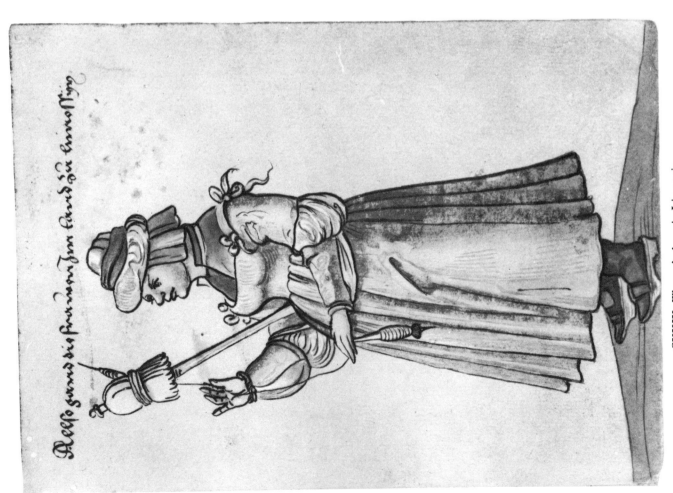

CXXIX. Women's dress in Limousin.

CXXXII. Girl carrying water in Hennegau.

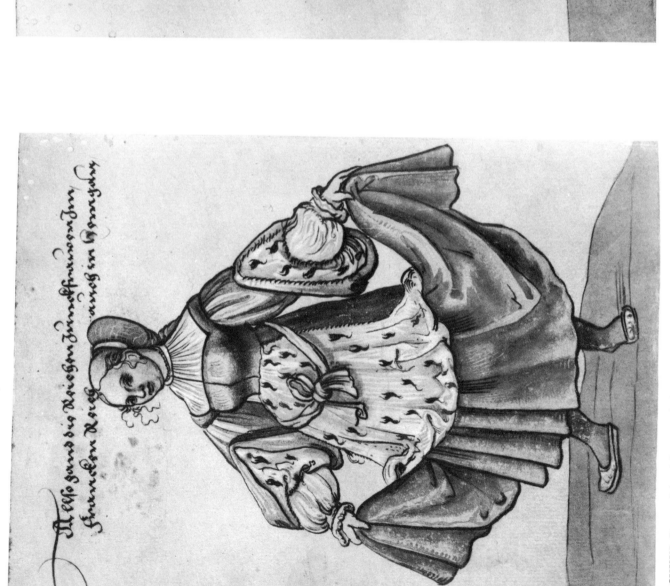

CXXXI. Dress of the rich unmarried women in France and Hennegau (Hainaut).

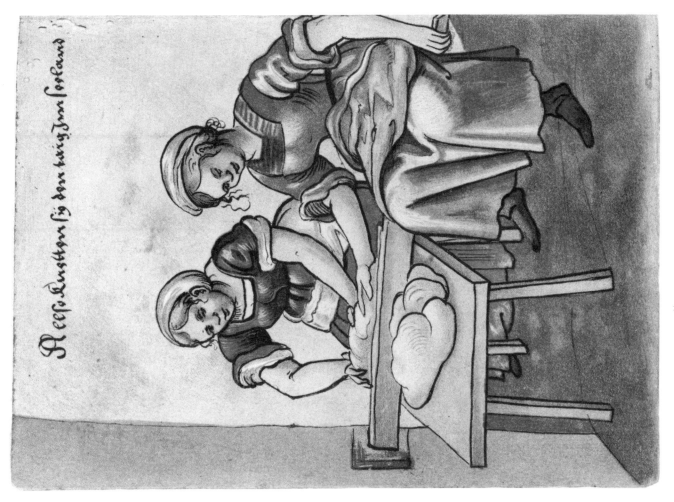

CXXXIV. Mixing dough in Zeeland.

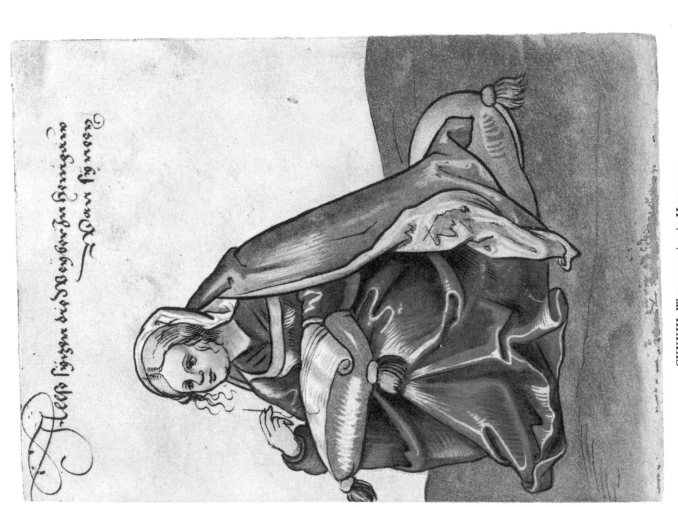

CXXXIII. Woman sewing in Hennegau.

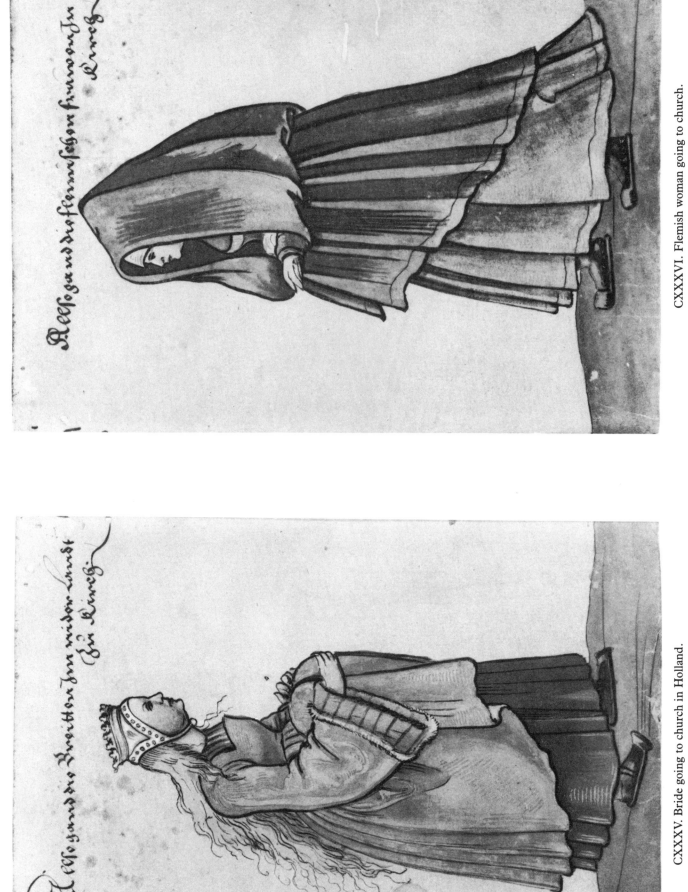

CXXXVI. Flemish woman going to church.

CXXXV. Bride going to church in Holland.

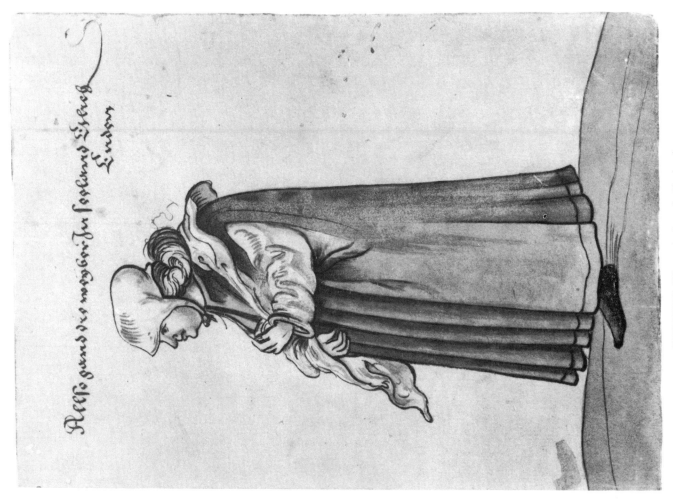

CXXXVIII. Women's dress in Zeeland.

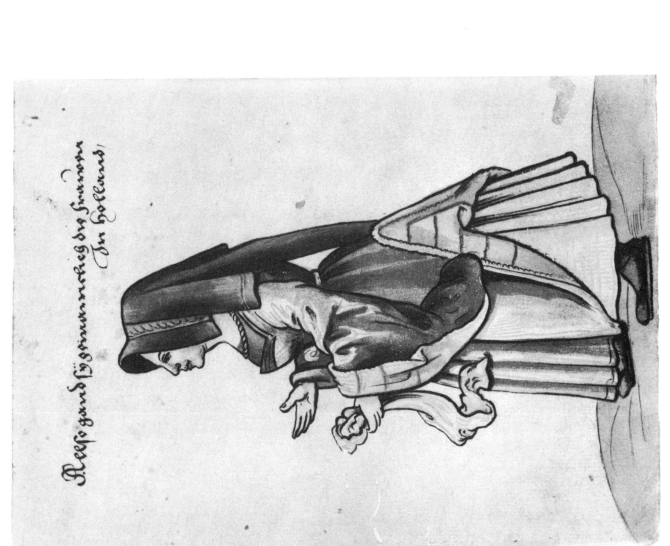

CXXXVII. Dutch women's dress.

CXXIX. Women's dress in Friesland.

CXL. Women's dress in Friesland.

CXLII. Former German dress.

CXLI. Former German dress.

CXLIV. Dress worn by the rich citizens of Genoa.

CXLIII. Dress worn by women in Vienna.

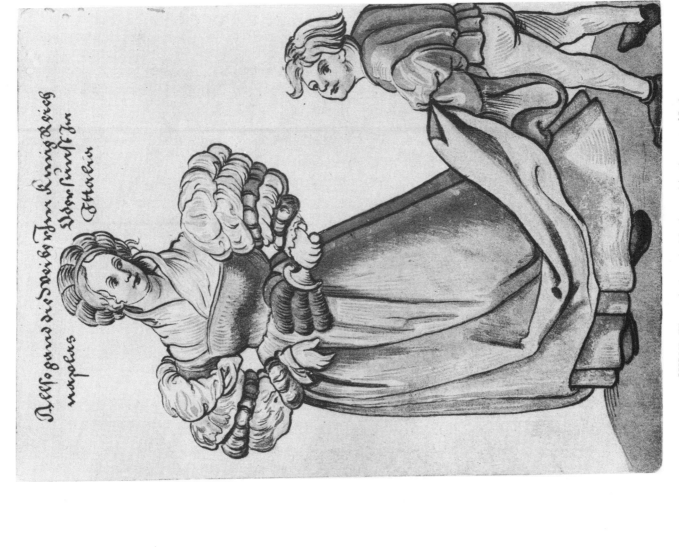

CXLVI. Women's dress in Naples and in the rest of Italy.

CXLV. Genoese woman going for a walk.

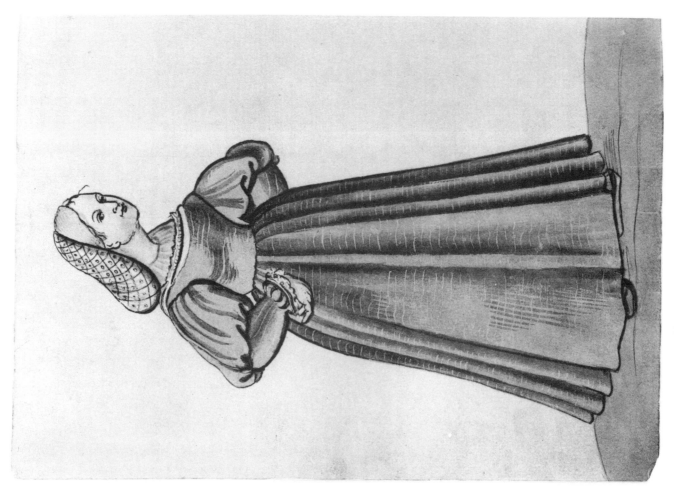

CXLVIII. Women's dress in Venice.

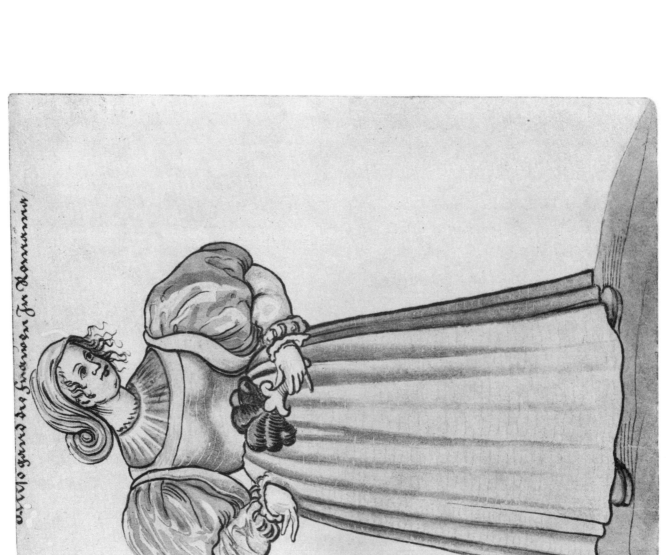

CXLVII. Women's dress in Romagna.

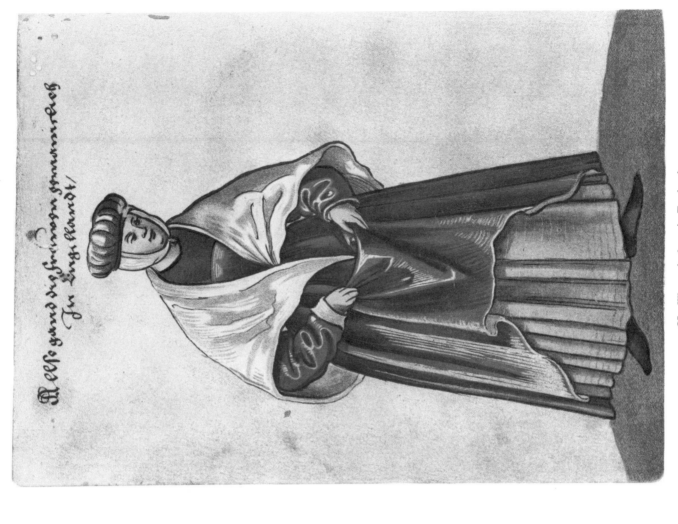

CXLIX. Men's dress in Venice.

CL. Women's dress in England.

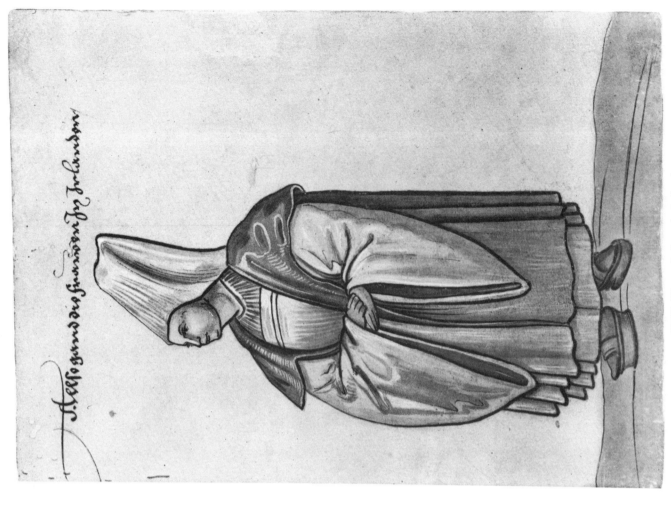

CLI. Dress worn by unmarried men in England.

CLII. Women's dress in Ireland.

CLIV. Dress worn by Portuguese women.

CLIII. Dress worn by the Portuguese.